CW00926202

Cruising

A Play in Two Acts

by

John Herdman

[signature: John Herdman]

diehard
Edinburgh

diehard
publishers
3 Spittal Street
Edinburgh
EH3 9DY

ISBN 0 946230 41 2

Cruising by John Herdman was first performed by Gallus Theatre Productions at Adam House Theatre, Edinburgh, on 2nd December 1996.

British Library Cataloguing in Publication Data
A catalog record for this book is
available from the British Library

The publisher ackowledges the financial assistance of the Scottish Arts Council in the publication of this volume.

Other books by John Herdman

Descent (Fiery Star Press, 1968)
A Truth Lover (Akros Publications, 1973)
Memoirs of my Aunt Minnie/Clapperton (Rainbow Books, 1974)
Pagan's Pilgrimage (Akros Publications, 1978)
Stories Short and Tall (Caithness Books, 1979)
Voice Without Restraint : Bob Dylan's Lyrics and their Background (Paul Harris, 1982; Delilah Books, New York, 1982)
Three Novellas (Polygon, 1987)
The Double in Nineteenth-Century Fiction (Macmillan,1990; St Martin's Press, New York, 1991)
Imelda and Other Stories (Polygon, 1993)
Ghostwriting (Polygon, 1996)

Other plays

Clapperton's Day (produced 1985)

Cruising

LIST OF CHARACTERS

Sir Hamish CADFOOT, Q.C.

Lady CADFOOT (Cynthia), his wife

Wee Davie COWMEADOW

Rev. James ARBUTHNOT

Captain Lindqvist

Ship's Doctor

Sonia, a barmaid

Bill, mate to Wee Davie

Waiters, barmen, serving wenches, etc.

SCENE: *The action takes place in Sir Hamish Cadfoot's house in Edinburgh; on board the cruising ship MS.* Saturn; *and in Copenhagen and Hamburg.*

TIME: *About the present.*

ACT I

SCENE I

The drawing room of the Cadfoots' house in the New Town, Edinburgh

Enter Sir Hamish Cadfoot. He is a well-dressed advocate aged about 55. He looks weary and dejected.

Sir Hamish: Hello, darling!

Cynthia: *(offstage)* Is that you darling?

Sir Hamish: Yes, darling, it's me.

Enter Cynthia. She is a few years younger than her husband.

Cynthia: You're home. *(He nods wearily). (anxiously)* Well ... tell me!

Sir Hamish: *(sighs)* The news isn't good, I'm afraid, darling. I'd better not beat about the bush. The affection has penetrated the epidermis and invaded the auricular chambers — the trachea may also be involved. Fraser says we have to be prepared for a spread throughout the epiglottal system. There's also evidence of cerebral anaemia, possibly linked to chronic degeneration of the central nervous system. The prognosis — the outlook, that is, darling — is ... well, it just isn't good.

Cynthia: *(after a pause)* I see. I suppose ... it couldn't just be your old diverticulitis again — you know ... the flatulence?

Sir Hamish: *(shakes his head)* Unh — unh. I wish it could.

Cynthia: No. Silly of me. *(pause)* Hamish, I think you should get a second opinion.

Sir Hamish: No point. The tests can't be wrong.

Cynthia: No, no, I suppose not. Still, there must be some treatment ... What can be done?

Sir Hamish: Oh, palliative treatment. Antibiotics, painkillers, analgesics, anti-spasmodics, anti-depressants, foot powder. *(He considers whether to say more)*. There *is* a possible surgical procedure, a very long shot ... I won't go into the details, darling, it would only distress you. It's a *very* long shot, and it might end up simply exacerbating the condition. Fraser doesn't recommend it, not at this stage. The fact is, it might even kill me.

Cynthia: *(earnestly)*. Hamish, I *still* think you should get a second opinion.

Sir Hamish: No. I trust Fraser implicitly.

Long silence.

Cynthia: Hamish, I think we should cry together.

Sir Hamish: No, no, not yet. There will be time ... indeed there will be time. Drink, darling? *(Cynthia nods and he pours drinks for them both. With a great effort pulls himself together)*. Well, that was the bad news. Now for the good news. As you know, darling, I'm not taking on any more cases, not at any rate for the present. *(Raises his glass)*. Here's to you, my love.

Cynthia: Happy days, darling ... I mean ... Oh, God! *(begins to cry) (He takes her in her arms)* Why did I have to say that? But it was always our toast, wasn't it, in the old days, the old happy days ...

Sir Hamish: Hush, hush, my sweet ... we must be brave! I was telling you the good news! As you know, I have a few cases for opinion which I must deal with in the next few days. Any new briefs I shall return. So — a week on Friday, we are off on a cruise, you and I! On the good ship *Saturn*, sailing from Leith. For twelve nights — the Northern Capitals! Oslo, Stockholm, Copenhagen — then on the way home, Hamburg and Amsterdam! Just the two of us. What do you say to that, eh?

Cynthia: *(drying her eyes)* Oh, Hamish, that's wonderful — just wonderful!

Sir Hamish: Yes, we'll have a marvellous holiday together, something for you always to remember, should the worst come to ... well, you know.

Cynthia: The worst. I know, darling, we have to face it.

Sir Hamish: Yes, Cynthia. We both have to be strong enough ... *(becoming confused)* for both of us. *(Takes a large drink of whisky and grows more expansive)* Scandinavia! I've always wanted to go there — the fjords, Elsinore, angst among the pine trees — do you remember those Bergman movies we used to see when we were students, darling? Women's faces full of vague hurt and betrayal, existential wolf-howls, Max von Sydow slurping out of a wooden bowl! Ah, youth! ... When we are young we think that time will last for ever, our time ... we don't know of any time but our own ... Then along comes a career, marriage, responsibilities, children — grandchildren, for God's sake! *(turns away and leans on a table). (brokenly)* Oh, God, Cynthia, how I want to watch little Samson growing up! *(The door bell rings).* Who the devil can that be at this time? We're not expecting anyone ... *(Answers door).*

Enter Wee Davie and Bill, carrying a door. Wee Davie is a wee man aged about 35. Exit Cynthia, in tears.

Davie: *(grinning, pleased with himself)* Got a door for ye, sir!

Sir Hamish: Oh good heavens! You said you'd give me advance warning!

Davie: Sorry, sir, didnae have your telephone number, that was the problem.

Sir Hamish: What? I've given it to you at least twice, I gave it to a girl at reception, then I gave it to the young joiner ...

Davie: Ah, well, that's no me! I'm the boss! See, I wouldnae ken where they'd written it down.

Sir Hamish: Oh well, you'd better come in. *(suspiciously)*. Where's the joiner?

Davie: Ay, well, I'm afraid young Stuart couldnae make it the night. See his sister's expecting a baby an' he had to take her to the hospital ... high blood pressure. Emergency, like.

Sir Hamish: Oh, good Lord!

Davie: I'm sorry, sir! I cannae prevent emergencies! Don't you worry, sir, Bill an' me'll hang it for ye, nae bother. Bill's juist no long oot o' his bed wi the flu, came specially like ... Got the hinges, Bill?

Bill: Naw, they're in the van.

Davie: In the van! Never mind, I'll get them.

Sir Hamish: Did you bring the handles?

Davie: Handles? No, nae handles, sir. See young Stuart was to get them at his work ...

Sir Hamish: *(Exasperated groan)*

Davie: Even if I'd got them sir , I'd no be able tae pit them on. See, young Stuart, he's the jiner, if Bill an' me tried tae pit them on we'd likely make a hash o' it. Ye're better waiting for young Stuart, sir. *(Exit)*.

Bill shrugs knowingly.

Sir Hamish: Oh, dear, dear. You know, he hasn't made a single arrangement with me over the past month that he's kept, not one, not a single one!

Bill: Ay. He's like that.

Sir Hamish: He assured me half a dozen times that he had the handles!

Bill: Ay, well, ye see ... He thought he had them ... but he hadnae.

4

Enter Wee Davie.

Davie: I've got the hinges, anyway, sir. We'll get this door hung for you the now, sir, then Bill an' me'll come back next week an' gie ye an hour's work on it, like the last time ... a bit sand an' a couple o coats of white vinegar, like.

Sir Hamish: What? You mean it's not finished? You promised me it'd be finished when you brought it!

Davie: Sorry, sir, it wasnae dry ... See if I'd tried tae work on it when it was wet, ye'd no be pleased with the results, sir.

Sir Hamish: But you assured me it *would* be dry!

Davie: Ah well, that was before Bill here went aff his work. See, the door wasnae taken oot the vat ...

Sir Hamish: *(giving up the struggle)* Never mind, then. Let's get the door up at least.

David and Bill turn the door right side up, upside down, both ways round, etc. They mutter together.

Davie: We've got a bit of a problem here, sir. The door's no the right size. It's a good inch an a half oot, sir. It's a' right vertically, like ...

Sir Hamish: I don't believe this!

Davie: I'm afraid ye've given us the wrong measurements, sir. Easily done, I'm no blamin' ye.

Sir Hamish: That's not possible. I measured it two or three times! *(shouts)* Cynthia! Can you bring down the tape measure please?

Enter Cynthia with tape measure.

Cynthia: There you are, love. Is that the right one?

Sir Hamish: Yes, yes. *(measuring)* This is completely out. This isn't what ... these aren't the measurements ...

Davie: That's what I'm sayin' sir. It's easily done. See Bill an' masel'll make a mistake sometimes, an we're daein' it every day!

Sir Hamish: I give up. *(turns away in despair)*.

Davie: We'll have tae take this back tae the shop, sir. Young Stuart'll be down at the beginning o' next week an' he'll cut it back ... let's see now ... he plays pool on a Monday ... We'll get it tae ye Tuesday, better make it Wednesday, sir, Wednesday, that's definite.

Sir Hamish: Oh no. I don't think that will be any good. We're going off on holiday at the end of next week, we'll be packing up, we won't want all this disturbance going on then ...

Davie: Ay, well, we're off frae the Friday wursels, sir, trades holidays, like.

Sir Hamish: Yes ... we'll just have to leave it, then. Leave it until the end of the month, I suppose.

Davie: Right ye are, sir. If you gie me a bell aboot the end o' the month, or I can gie ye a ring, whatever suits yersel, sir ...

Sir Hamish: I'll get in touch with you, Mr Cowmeadow.

Davie: Very good, sir. I'm sorry aboot a' this, but thae things happen sir, ye ken yersel ...

Sir Hamish: That's all right ... good night, then.

Davie and Bill: G'night, sahr! *(Exeunt Wee Davie and Bill. Sir Hamish slumps in a chair, physically and emotionally exhausted. Cynthia comes up and strokes his hair tenderly).*

Cynthia: That must have been terrible for you, darling.

Sir Hamish: It wasn't the best timing in the world, was it? Still, you can't help laughing ... What an utterly hopeless little man he is! Did you notice the way he tried to blame the size of the door on me? I gave him the correct measurements — he's just bloody useless!

Cynthia: And the other one's black eye — did you see that?

Sir Hamish: Oh yes — he's supposed to have been in his bed with 'the flu' for the past two days — I'll bet he never collected that there!

Cynthia: Well, not with 'the flu' — but with a floosie, perhaps! *(They laugh condescendingly).* Oh, darling, it's wonderful to be able to laugh, isn't it? Even at a time like this.

Sir Hamish: Yes ... even at a time like this.

Cynthia: Put it *all* out of your mind, Hamish — the illness, the doors, the joiners, the lot! Soon we'll be far, far away from all that ... Who knows what good the bracing northern air might do you!

Sir Hamish: Yes, Fraser said there was much to be said for fine air ... who knows? You know, if I hadn't paid for the door already I'd have told the little shit to piss off.

Cynthia: *Forget* it, Hamish. Don't give him another thought — he's just not worth it. Think of the *Saturn* and the Northern Capitals.

The door bell rings.

Sir Hamish: Oh, good God, I don't believe this!

Cynthia: He's come back for the door, darling. See — he's left it behind!

Sir Hamish: This is beyond belief.

He answers the door. Enter Wee Davie and Bill.

Davie: Forgot the door, sir.

Sir Hamish: *(laughing weakly)* On you come then. Perhaps this chapter of accidents will now come to an end.

Davie: It'll be right when we get it back tae ye sir, I can promise you that. Awright, Bill?

In manoeuvering the door they knock a priceless vase off a table. It is smashed to smithereens. Cynthia shrieks. Brief tableau.

Davie: Sorry aboot that, sir.

Cynthia: *(sobbing)* Mummy's vase! You clumsy bloody oafs!

Sir Hamish: *(with some detachment)* This is too much, Mr Cowmeadow. That was a priceless and irreplaceable work of art. This really is the end.

Davie: *(hesitantly)* Insurance'll cover it, like ...

Tableau.

Other **diehard** drama

Klytemnestra's Bairns, Bill Dunlop
Cutpurse/Once in Beaucaire, Bill Dunlop
Hare and Burke, Owen Dudley Edwards
Gang Doun wi a Sang, a play about William Soutar,
by Joy Hendry
Port and Lemon, the mystery behind Sherlock Holmes
/Laird of Samoa, John Cargill Thompson
Cheap and Tearful/Feel Good, John Cargill Thompson
*Hamlet II: Prince of Jutland/ Macbeth Speaks/ An English
Education*, John Cargill Thompson
Everything in the Garden and other plays,
by John Cargill Thompson
*What Shakespeare Missed/Romeo & Juliet: Happily Never
After/The Marvellous Boy/Cock-a-doodle-do!*
by John Cargill Thompson.
A Matter of Conviction/Parting Shot/When the Rain Stops,
by John Cargill Thompson
The Lord Chamberlain's Sleepless Nights, a collection
of plays by John Cargill Thompson

plays in latin

Alcestis & Medea by George Buchanan

SCENE II

On board MS. Saturn — the deck. Sir Hamish and Cynthia are leaning on the rail.

Cynthia: Oh, isn't this wonderful, Hamish! We're on our way.

Sir Hamish: And what a day for it! Who would think the old Firth of Forth could ever look so beautiful? All the spatial relationships, you know, the positions of the islands, seem so different when you're sailing down the Forth. That must be Fidra, and there's the Lamb ... I wonder whether we'll pass close to the Isle of May. I've always wanted to get a close look at it, see the bird colonies.

Cynthia: I once sailed round the Bass. It was a half-term weekend, I think.

Sir Hamish: There's North Berwick. Edinburgh seems so far away — Oslo next stop. Pity the beer's so expensive in Norway ... Oh my God. Keep looking ahead, Cynthia. Straight ahead.

Cynthia: *(looking ahead — whispers)* What is it, Hamish? Have you seen someone we know? *(giggles)* It's not the Macraes, is it?

Enter Wee Davie, in blazer, yachting cap and cravat. He is about to wander past, but suddenly recognises them.

Davie: So this is where ye go for yer holidays! Turn-up for the books eh? How-do-you-do, sahr! Very glad to see you, Lady Cadfoot! Gettin' away frae lousy-door merchants, eh? Who'd hae guessed it, though!

Sir Hamish: Who indeed! Er ... never thought a cruise would be *your* cup of tea, Mr Cowmeadow.

Davie: Well, see, I won it in a prize, like. Spot the Ba', ken? Just thought I'd gie it a spin, an' my number come up, in a manner o' speakin' — so I thought, well, why no? Get away frae it a', eh?

Cynthia: You were jolly lucky ... Is your wife with you?

Davie: Naw, naw. The prize was fur two, right enough, but see my wife's went aff, last year there, she's puntin' about wi' a taxi driver ... so I'm fancy-free. I thought about takin' a girl friend, right enough, but they says ye can take the money instead of the second fare, so I thought well why not, mebbe get another wee holiday later on, eh?

Sir Hamish: Wise decision, I'd have thought.

Davie: An' what aboot yersels? Always fancied a cruise, have ye?

Sir Hamish: Why, yes, one to Scandinavia, anyway. We've been on one or two to other parts, we both like the sea. And then I haven't been too well, and the doctor recommended some fresh North Sea breezes!

Davie: Aw, I'm sorry to hear that..what's the trouble, like?

Sir Hamish: *(loftily)* Oh, it's an extremely rare condition, no one's heard of it ... *(hesitates)* It's known as postural-sacral redundancy syndrome, actually.

Davie: Get away! That's what my auntie had ... the very same!

Sir Hamish: *(incredulous)* Really? Are you sure? It's really very rare.

Davie: *(considers)* Is there epiglottal involvement?

Sir Hamish: Er ... yes ... yes ... as a matter of fact there is.

Davie: *(nods knowingly)* Ay. It was the very same wi' my auntie. The very same. Mind you, wi my auntie it was intae the cerebellum an' a'. Ay, I mind when she tellt my uncle, "Hughie, I've got posterior-sacral redundancy syndrome", he says, "Ay", he says, "that means if ye sit on yer arse all day yer legs'll eventually drap aff!" He was tryin' tae cheer her up, like. *Silence.* So the doctor's recommended sea air, eh?

Sir Hamish: *(jocularly)* He thought it might keep me going for a bit yet!

Davie: Ay, even if ye get anither year or two, like, it'd always be somethin', eh?

Cynthia: *(protesting)* Oh, Hamish's doctor is very confident that the treatment he's getting will be effective.

Davie: Ay, that's what they tellt my auntie ... Mind you, she was an older person than yersel. *(aware of consternation)* I'm sorry, am ah speakin' outa turn?

Sir Hamish: Oh, no, that's all right..one gets used to it, you know, one gets hardened!

Awkward pause.

Davie: Aw well, I'll better away an' unpack my bags. I'll see ye's later, eh? *(Exit).*

Cynthia: Oh, my God, Hamish. That was ghastly. Just ghastly. *(begins to cry)*

Sir Hamish: He's a bit of a rough diamond, isn't he? I'm sure he means well enough, though.

Cynthia: You can't just dismiss it like that! He's going to be hanging around us for the whole trip now! Oh, darling, it just isn't fair! Our la ... I mean our *wonderful* holiday together — what a beastly trick for fate to play on us!

Sir Hamish: *(irritated)* Oh, don't make so much of it, Cynthia! It's a big enough boat, I'm sure we'll be able to keep out of his way easily enough. And if it doesn't become obvious to him that he isn't wanted, we'll just have to make it clearer, won't we? That he's *persona non grata.*

Cynthia: He was so bloody familiar!

Sir Hamish: Well, that class are often like that nowadays, you know. He probably thinks that because we're all on holiday it's all right.

Cynthia: But it isn't all right! It just isn't. This is the man who smashed Mummy's vase! Her pride and joy — she was talking about it on the day she died!

Sir Hamish: Forget it, Cynthia.

Enter Captain Lindqvist.

Captain: Sir Hamish, Lady Cadfoot, how are you! We met before, on the *Pluto*, you remember? Yes, yes. It is so good to have you aboard. We are indeed privileged.

Cynthia: And we are so happy to be with you, Captain.

Captain: And the weather is kind, is it not? I think it remains like this all the trip.

Cynthia: Oh Captain, you can guarantee the weather!

Captain: On my own patch of sea, you know, Lady Cadfoot. I do my best.

Cynthia: I know it's going to be a very special voyage.

Captain: *(bows)* My crew and I will do all in our power to make it so. And I saw you were talking just now with Mr Cowmeadow, our Prizewinner. A very important passenger, you know.

Sir Hamish: Ah, yes, as a matter of fact we have — how shall I put it? — rubbed up against him before. At home.

Captain: Ah, so you have made his acquaintance before? How very fortunate, for I think — yes, I am sure! — that you sit at same table in the dining saloon.

Sir Hamish: Oh — really? That should be interesting.

Captain: So! I shall see you at my party tomorrow evening. I think it will be fun.

Cynthia: We shall so much look forward to that, Captain. *(Captain bows and exits).* Hamish, we're going to have to change our table.

Sir Hamish: That's not on, I'm afraid, Cynthia: You know the lists are always publicly displayed. It would be far too obvious — poor chap'd realise at once. You just can't do that sort of thing. Much as I'd love to.

Cynthia: So we just accept the total ruination of our holiday? Share a table with the man who smashed Mummy's vase? *That's* not on, Hamish.

Sir Hamish: Oh, Cynthia, don't be so negative! I'm prepared to make the best of it and so must you. He's not really *that* bad ... all right, he is. But we must make it our business to civilise him. Look upon it as a challenge, my dear. You might end up falling in love with him. *(chortles).*

Cynthia: I don't really find that very funny, Hamish, especially in ... in the circumstances.

Sir Hamish: Oh, for God's sake!

Cynthia: In fact, I find it very hurtful. Here I am trying to make this a wonderful holiday for you, and all you can do is make cheap jokes at my expense.

12

Sir Hamish: It was a joke, Cynthia, possibly cheap, I don't know, I've never been very good at assessing the market value of jokes, but not intended to be at your expense ...

Cynthia: Like hell it wasn't!

Sir Hamish: ... And as for the holiday, I was under the impression that *I'd* arranged it.

Cynthia: Oh yes, you arranged it, so that your precious syndrome could be the subject of conversation from Leith to Helsinki. I'm sick of your boring syndrome, and your selfishness and pompous self-importance. Sick, sick, sick of them — up to here!

Sir Hamish: Cynthia — have you gone crazy? Are you seriously suggesting that I've conjured up my illness to get attention? This is appalling — it's unworthy of you! I can't believe what I'm hearing!

Cynthia: Well even if you haven't, it would certainly be in character if you had! Sit with your bloody Mr Cowmeadow if you want to, you can talk about your symptoms and his auntie's from Helsinki to Hell if it turns you on — I won't be joining you! *(Storms off)*.

Sir Hamish: *(shouts after her)*. We're not going to Helsinki, Cynthia!

Utterly deflated, he leans dejectedly on the rail for some time. Enter Wee Davie.

Davie: Hamish, I just seen your good lady gae doon the corridor in an awfae hurry, there — ye've no fallen oot, like?

Sir Hamish: Oh, just a small difference of opinion — you know how it is. Perceptive of you.

Davie: Ay, I know how it is a' right, I know how it is.

Sir Hamish: Yes ... isn't Scotland looking beautiful today as we draw away from her. I often wonder, you know, why we go abroad when our own land has so much to offer. But then Scotland always looks most beautiful when one is leaving her.

Davie: We sell ourselves short, Hamish. See the other week there I was up Perth way an' I went for a stroll up a hill, it was a beautiful day, blue sky, sun shinin' an' that, and there was this wee gap in the hills, an' I got a glisk like, juist a wee view ye understand, of a' these white towers shinin' faur away in the sun through this gap ... I'm tellin ye, Hamish, it was that beautiful, it was that white an' shinin', it coulda been the towers of Camelot.

Sir Hamish: How splendid ... what was it, David?

Davie: It wis Dundee, 's a matter of fact. But there you are.

Sir Hamish: *(turns to him)* David, that was very evocative — you don't mind if I call you David? — you painted a very lovely picture there. I believe we're sharing a table in the dining saloon — you know, I think we're going to have a lot to talk about! *(confidentially)* And I'll tell you something else. I was actually jolly pleased when you smashed that vase — I've always hated it.

Davie: *(modestly)* Ach well, dae wur best, ken.

SCENE III

The Dining Saloon. The same evening.

Sir Hamish, Lady Cadfoot, Wee Davie and the Rev. James Arbuthnot are already seated at table.

Arbuthnot: Lord, out of your abundant store you have given us good things to eat, and water from your eternal springs to slake our thirst. You have granted us fine weather and a fair breeze and have set us before you at the table of fellowship and mutual love. Lord, we invoke your blessing on this ship and all who sail in her. May the wind of your Holy Spirit fill our sails and your Word be our guide and our only support throughout our voyage. As we journey towards you in Hope, fill our hearts and minds with that hunger which no earthly food may satisfy, and that thirst which can be slaked only from the well of your living waters. Be our lighthouse and our lifeboat in all the storms of life; guide us, guard us and keep us safe from all shipwreck until that day when, our robes washed white from every stain of sin in the saving blood of your Son, we enter at last into our everlasting port. We ask this through Jesus Christ, Our Lord. Amen.

General relief, embarrassed pause.

Well, well, isn't this delightful. It's always a bit of a worry, isn't it, whom one is going to end up sitting with on these occasions. But I think we're all going to 'click' as they say. I'm Jim Arbuthnot. *(extends his hand).*

Sir Hamish: My name is Hamish — Hamish Cadfoot, and this is my wife, Cynthia. *(How-do-you-do's are exchanged).* And this is Mr David Cowmeadow.

Davie: Glad tae meet you, Reverend.

Arbuthnot: *(to Hamish)* I beg your pardon — did you say your name was Catfood?

Sir Hamish: *(laughing ruefully)* No, no, Cadfoot — the other way round!

Arbuthnot: Ah, Cadfoot! I'm so sorry.

Davie: I expect you'll get a lot of that, Hamish. You have my very sincere sympathy. Wi' a name like Cowmeadow, I ken whit it's like!

Cynthia: Gosh yes, *it is* unusual!

Davie: There's an interesting story attached to that name, as a matter or fact, Cynthia. It seems there was a boy owned a meadow an' he pit some cows intae it, so they ca'd him Cowmeadow ... So that was actually the origin of the name.

Cynthia: Gosh — how fascinating. *(Silence)*.

Enter Waiter, who serves the first course.

Davie: May I say that I admired your grace, Reverend? The power o' language, nothing like it.

Arbuthnot: *(pleased)* Ah, well — like all of God's gifts, it can be used for good or ill.

Cynthia: Yes — look at how all those politicians abuse it! You can't believe a word they say. I don't trust *any* of them, I don't care what party they belong to, I have no faith in any of them.

Sir Hamish: It's the civil servants that get to me — all that gobbledegook! Obfuscation by the barrowload. And the council officials! 'We're talking about this' and 'we're talking that', 'at this moment in time', 'on behalf of' when they mean 'on the part of' — 'a disgraceful action on behalf of the Government'. Not to mention journalists — floating participles — 'gender' when they mean 'sex'! Ugh!

Davie: There's piles of folk in Scotland like that, Hamish. Wee nyaffs.

Sir Hamish: *(clears his throat)* Shall we order some wine? Mr Arbuthnot, would you care to join us?

Arbuthnot: *(holds up his palms)* Not for me, thank you.

Sir Hamish: Er ... David, what about yourself?

Davie: Ay, why not Hamish? I'll join ye's. Nice bottle of Beaujolais, mebbe?

Sir Hamish: Well, let's see, let's see. Waiter! *(Enter Waiter)*. We'll have two bottles of No. 29 please. Cabin 14.

Davie: Drinks'll be on me eftir dinner, then.

Cynthia: And what made you decide to cruise on the *Saturn,* Mr Arbuthnot?

Arbuthnot: Ah well, Mrs Cadfoot, I was badly in need of a break: you see, my wife ...

Davie: *(nudges him) Lady* Cadfoot, Reverend, Cynthia's a Lady, like ...

Arbuthnot: *(confused)* Oh, I do beg your pardon, I hadn't realised ...

Cynthia: Oh, no, not at all, Mr Arbuthnot, you weren't to know ... You were saying?

Arbuthnot: *(sighs)* Yes, yes ... I lost Mrs Arbuthnot at Christmas, it was a heavy blow. That she should have been taken from me at Christmas, of all times, after forty years of companionship and happiness, it seemed so cruel — it quite shook my faith for a time, but, God be praised, I'm over that now.

Cynthia: Oh, we *do* understand, life *does* seem cruel sometimes ... Hamish, you know, is *very* ill.

Davie: *(confidentially, to Arbuthnot)* It's terminal, like.

Sir Hamish: *(piqued)* No, David, it's not terminal. My illness is incurable, yes, it is perhaps fatal, but it is not yet terminal. David, I suspect that you are labouring under a misapprehension as to the meaning of the word 'terminal'. A disease is described as terminal when it has reached its terminal, that is, its *final* stages. It doesn't mean that you are certainly going to die of this disease, sometime; it means that you are going to die very, very soon — like this week.

Davie: *(crestfallen)* Ay. There's a lot of folk don't realise that.

Sir Hamish: Yes, David there are, and until about ten seconds ago you were one of them.

The wine is served.

Cynthia: Actually, I agree with David ...

Sir Hamish: *(trying to control fury)* If you agree with David, my dear, that merely proves that you are *both* wrong.

17

Arbuthnot: Come, come, let us agree to differ then — let charity and good humour prevail!

Cynthia: Thank you, Mr Arbuthnot. I think you expressed yourself quite correctly, Davie.

Arbuthnot: *(intervening swiftly)* And then I'm most interested in the Lutheran Church, I hope to be visiting a number of churches at our various ports of call.

Davie: The Lutherans — ay, well. Enough said. The Greek Orthodox, though, they're somethin' else! See that Epiclesis, eh? See when the boy invokes the Holy Spirit — I seen that in Cyprus. Magic, eh, Reverend?

Arbuthnot: Yes, indeed. I think that would be the word for it.

Sir Hamish: *(satirical but genial)* You're a bit of a theologian, are you, David?

Davie: Ach well, no whit ye'd actually call a theologian — I used tae be intae Christology an' that, ken.

Cynthia: Is there any reason why David shouldn't be interested in theology, Hamish?

Sir Hamish: I'm sorry — I wasn't aware that I'd suggested he shouldn't be. I thought I'd merely asked him whether he was.

Cynthia: It seemed to me that that was what you were suggesting.

The main course is served.

Now, can I help everyone to vegetables. Carrots, Mr Arbuthnot? And what about a few shallots? They do look delicious.

Davie: Ay ... think we'll ca' ye The Lady of Shallots!

Cynthia: Oh, Davie, that's disgraceful! *(laughing coyly)* You're a punster in addition to all your other talents.

Davie: Naw, naw, I was only kiddin'. But on the subject of theology, there is one question I would like very seriously to put to your good self, Mr Arbuthnot.

Arbuthnot: Oh please, call me Jim, for goodness' sake.

Davie: O.K., Jim, fair enough. The question I would like to put to you is this: what is your personal view, Jim, about the Theotokos?

Arbuthnot: *(highly taken aback)* Er ... the Theotokos?

Davie: Ay. The Godbearer. The Mother of God, like.

Arbuthnot: Well ... what is my view of it? Well, now, that is indeed a question.

Davie: Ay, there's a lot of folk take exception to that phrase.

Arbuthnot: Well, I suppose, if pressed, I would probably admit to being one of their number.

Davie: So what is your objection, Jim? I'm asking this very sincerely.

Arbuthnot: Well, I suppose I must try to answer ... if, that is, our friends would not object? — it seems perhaps a little deep for the dinner table, even a little controversial ...

Sir Hamish: *(struggling with astonishment)* No, no, please — don't mind us ...

Arbuthnot: Why, then, Mary is, of course, the mother of Our Lord, no doubt of that; but to say that she is the Mother of God ...

Davie: Ay, well, Jesus is God, no?

Arbuthnot: Assuredly, Jesus is God, God the Son ...

Davie: Right, Jim. Jesus is God an' Mary's his Maw, excuse ma French, so Mary's the Mother of God. Am I right or am I wrang?

Arbuthnot: Ah, now, hold on, David, hold on. In our Lord Jesus Christ there are two natures, human and Divine. Now as to the human nature, the Virgin Mary is undoubtedly his mother. But as to the Divine ...

Davie: *(eagerly)* Ay, now we're gettin tae it, Jim. Two natures but one person, Jim. Am I right or am I wrang? Two natures in one Person, OK?

Arbuthnot: Yes, yes, indeed, that is the true position.

Davie: Awright. Two natures indivisibly present in one Person. Nae division between them, mind. *(triumphantly)* Right then. Way I see it, a wumman can only be the mother of a person, she cannae be the mother of a nature — disnae mean anything, that.

So she's the mother of a person an' that person — as ye've admitted yersel, Jim — is God. So Mary's the Mother of God. *Quod erat demonstrandum*, excuse ma French.

Arbuthnot: *(reluctantly)* Well, put like that I suppose ... I can't immediately think ...

Davie: Say nae mair. No offence, Jim, OK? No offence. Put it there, pal. *(offers his hand to shake. Nonplussed, Arbuthnot takes it. Pause).*

Sir Hamish: Well, this saltimbocca is delicious, I must say.

Davie: Wine's no bad an' a'. Slanjy vah.

Cynthia: Someone told us recently that claret should never be drunk with veal. I disagree with him, profoundly. Who was it, again, Hamish, who told us that?

Sir Hamish: It was Brian, I think. Brian Fowler-Gibbon.

Davie: Fowler-Gibbon — what sort of a name's that? 'A fouler gibbon I never did see'! ...

Cynthia: *(admiringly)* Now, Davie, that's not very nice — you're playing to the gallery now. It would be very easy to make up a nasty rhyme about *your* name, you know.

Davie: OK, Cynthia, be my guest.

Cynthia: How do you mean, Davie?

Davie: Go on, make up a rhyme aboot ma name. You said it would be easy.

Cynthia: Oh , all right! *(thinks)*

There was a young fellow called Cowmeadow ...

Long pause.

I can't think of a rhyme!

Davie: Cynthia, I am disappointed in you. I thought better of your poetic resourcefulness, let us say. Never mind, hen. Your job on this voyage is to look beautiful.

Cynthia: Oh, you chauvinist!

Davie: Naw, but seriously. You said earlier that you were a grannie, Cynthia?

Cynthia: Oh, yes indeed. Our little Samson is just three months old.

Davie: Right then. You are the candidate chosen by this table, Cynthia — I think we can a' agree — to be our entrant for the Glamorous Grannies competition. To be held on Thursday evening in the Blue Lounge there. I seen it on the noticeboard.

Cynthia: *(delighted)* Oh, Davie, don't be ridiculous! I couldn't possibly!

Davie: Jim, I appeal to you! Did you ever see a grannie mair glamorous than this yin?

Arbuthnot: Well now, David, you are putting me on the spot! Chivalry demands that I say 'no'. And 'no' I do say, not because chivalry demands it, but because it is true.

Davie: There ye are then! You cannae refuse the minister!

Cynthia: You're all so persuasive!

Sir Hamish: At the risk of putting a damper on all this ardour, I agree with you, Cynthia, that it would scarcely be appropriate.

Cynthia: *(furious)* Oh, I know that *you* don't consider me glamorous!

Sir Hamish: Cynthia, that is scarcely the point ...

Cynthia: I notice that you don't deny it, though!

Sir Hamish: Cynthia, you are glamorous. You are very, very glamorous. I lack the resources of language to do justice to the full extent of your glamour. All right? That established, the point which I was trying to make was that you would be detracting from your great natural dignity were you to enter this competition.

Cynthia: I don't see why!

Sir Hamish: Darling, you said yourself, to begin with, that you couldn't possibly.

Cynthia: That was just a figure of speech — I hadn't really thought about it then.

Davie: Come oan, Hamish, let her, juist for a laugh, like!

Arbuthnot: I don't think there need be any great loss of dignity in such an innocent proceeding, Sir Hamish.

Sir Hamish: You gentlemen can afford to think that, it's not your wife who is aspiring to glamorous grandmotherhood. However, I suppose there is nothing I can do to prevent you, Cynthia, if you are determined. You will have to forgive me if I absent myself from the great occasion.

Cynthia: *(sarcastically)* Oh, I shall put a brave face on it, Hamish. But my two good friends will be there to support me, I hope?

Davie: You can count on me, Cynthia. Wouldnae miss it for anything.

Arbuthnot: Likewise, Lady Cadfoot. The honour of the table demands our presence. Let us drink to your success.

They drink, Sir Hamish with a show of reluctance and distaste.

SCENE IV

Three days later: The deck.

Enter Cynthia. She looks around cautiously.
Enter Wee Davie.

Davie: We-ell! How glamorous our gorgeous grannie does look today! Good morning, Cynthia.

Cynthia: Oh, Davie! Isn't it a wonderful morning! It feels like that to me, anyway, even if the sun is hiding behind a cloud. I won! I still can't believe it. What a magical evening it was, wasn't it? And I owe it all to you, Davie. I'd have been far, far too diffident ever to have entered off my own bat. Thank you, my sweet man.

Davie: See you an' me, Cynthia, we're the two winners on this boat, eh? Somethin' in common.

Cynthia: Yes, we are, and I could name one loser! ... Oh I shouldn't say that, I know. It's very unkind of me. But Davie, Hamish has been making me feel worthless for a quarter of a century now, and I've just realised that it's him that's worthless, not me. Last night I emerged from the shadow of worthlessness in which I have been . shrouded. Shrouded, that's the word. And now I have emerged to new life. All thanks to you.

She kisses him on the cheek.

Davie: Cynthia, you are a very lovely lady. You can be confident that I speak in all sincerity when I say that you have no valid grounds for considering yourself worthless.

Cynthia: Oh, thank you, Davie! You understand so much. Davie, we must never let Hamish discover what happened in Oslo.

Davie: (*puzzled*) Eh ... what was that, then? ... It's a' a bit hazy, like ...

Cynthia: Oh, Davie, you know, you can't fool me. We both know. Not that we did anything wrong, it was all entirely

23

innocent ... still, it was *there*, wasn't it?

Davie: Oh ay, Cynthia, it was there a'right.

Cynthia: *(hesitating)* Davie, Hamish is dying ... Oh, what am I saying? I don't believe that, I mustn't believe it. But it's true all the same. Davie ... Oh, here he comes!

She composes herself. Enter Sir Hamish, looking woebegone.

Sir Hamish: I feel appalling. Just absolutely appalling.

Davie: Would ye care for a Kwell, Hamish? I've got some down in my cabin there.

Sir Hamish: Thank you, Davie, but what is happening to my body will not yield to any Kwell. The pain is everywhere, today. It's in my feet, my stomach, my skin, my hair, my soul ... Yes, my soul also. The trouble is in my soul today.

Davie: That's what my auntie used to say.

Cynthia: Hamish, the sun is shining ...

Sir Hamish: Is it? I can't see it myself.

Cynthia: ... we are sailing down the Kattegat, the scenery is breathtaking, soon we shall be in Copenhagen ... I know you are ill, darling, but don't you think that if you looked on the positive side you might feel a little better — perhaps even very much better?

Davie: *(sings)* Wonderful, wonderful Copenhagen ...

Sir Hamish: Davie, please. Cynthia, I'm sure that the day must appear wonderful the morning after one has been officially declared the most glamorous grandmother on board the good ship *Saturn*. My situation is otherwise, far otherwise. A fortnight ago, you may remember, I had occasion to seek the advice of Dr Malcolm Fraser, consultant physician. He told me ...

Cynthia: Oh, he's going to start talking about his horrible boring syndrome again! I can't bear it! I just can't bear it, Hamish! Could you not just for one moment forget about yourself ... Oh, I just can't trust myself to say any more! *(She storms off)*.

Long silence. They lean on rail.

Sir Hamish: You see what I have to put up with, Davie.

Davie: Women are a' the same, Hamish.

Sir Hamish: Yes ... It must have been awful for you when Marlene went off with that taxi-driver.

Davie: Ay, ach well, you have tae be philosophical aboot thae things, eh, Hamish? Mair fish in the sea, an' that. She'd got awfae thick in the leg an' a', Marlene. Still, it was a blow, awright.

Sir Hamish: But you came through, Davie. You survived.

Davie: That's the name o' the game, Hamish. Survival.

Sir Hamish: *(sighs deep and long)* Yes ...

Davie: *(understanding)* Sorry, I shouldnae have said that, Hamish. Didnae think, like.

Sir Hamish: *(with a deep look)* Davie, I haven't had all that many friends in my life. Real friends, I mean. They're hard to come by. You and I, we've only known one another a few days ... other than professionally, of course. *(laughs awkwardly)* But I think you have a very deep understanding of the way I'm feeling.

Davie: Ach well, dae wur best, ken.

Sir Hamish: I suppose, Davie, I have been what is called a success in life. As the world sees it, that is. I am respected in my profession, spoken of highly, even *(satirically)* tipped for higher things. I have a beautiful wife — have I not, Davie? — children of whom I am quietly proud, and now a grandchild — little Samson, you know. I have never known material want. I have a lovely home — you've seen it yourself, Davie ...

Davie: Ay, once you get thae doors in, Hamish, it'll be something special then, eh? See an old hoose like yours, Hamish, disnae look right withoot the original doors. I seen one the other week there, no faur frae where ye stay yersel, the doors had been painted a kinda turquoise, it was really awfae, no in keepin' like, understand my meaning? But see thae doors I got for you, those are original-type doors ...

Sir Hamish: Yes, yes of course ... the point I was making, though, is ... I don't want to appear over-satirical about those advantages I was laying before you. I do value them. I value them highly. They are the goals towards which I have been striving, all my life. Never questioned them. Life just went on in its predetermined track: all's well enough, all will no doubt continue to be well enough. Then, one fine day, one doesn't feel so well, nothing you can put your finger on, a vague ache here, a little weakness there, a bit depressed, you wonder if it's the male menopause. You go to the doctor, and — wham! There he is, staring you straight in the face, the one you've never wanted to think about, to acknowledge even — there he is, saying, "Here I am. Right beside you. Very, very close. Coming for you soon." Death.

Davie: The grim reaper, eh, Hamish? Comes tae us a'.

Sir Hamish: Yes — you understand, don't you, Davie? You have an insight into these things — if only Cynthia could see it as you do!

Davie: Way I see it, Hamish, Cynthia's denyin' your illness. Disnae want to tae face it, like. She's angry with the syndrome, like, but you cannae really be angry wi' a syndrome, it cannae answer back, ken, ye cannae argue wi' a syndrome. So she's angry wi' you instead, for havin' the syndrome. Awright? Understand my meaning?

Sir Hamish: Perfectly! Perfectly! It fits! Davie, you're a very remarkable person, you know. You are capable of the most delicate yet penetrating perceptions ... Davie ... Oh, God, here comes the minister. I'm not up to that this morning. I'm sorry, Davie, I'll see you later. *(Exit)*.

Enter the Rev. James Arbuthnot.

Arbuthnot: Well, David, a fine healthy morning, is it not? That was a fascinating conversation we were having last night — about the Arian controversy. Quite fascinating. I had never seen that quite so clearly before, you know, that Arius envisaged the Trinity as three entirely separate beings, not sharing the same nature or essence.

Davie: Ay, well, the way I understand it, Jim — correct me if I'm wrang — Arius seen God as unique and transcendent, OK? Right, then, he says — I'm no sayin' I agree wi'him, mind — if God imparted his substance, that'd make him divisible and subject tae change. Stands tae reason, according to Arius. So the Son has tae be a creature, wi' a beginning, like. Born outside time, mind, he wisnae denyin' that, but 'there was a time when he was not'.

Arbuthnot: *(pondering)* Yes, yes ... For Arius, then, co-eternality must imply two self-existent principles?

Davie: Either that, or rank Sabellianism. Horns of a dilemma, eh, Jim?

Arbuthnot: Tell, me David, if you don't mind me asking, how did you become so very proficient in theology?

Davie: Ach well, I used tae work as a barman, like.

Arbuthnot: Ah! *(considers)* David, I think you get on well with our friends, the Cadfoots?

Davie: Oh ay, we get on smashin'.

Arbuthnot: That's what I thought. I'm rather concerned about them, David. We both know, of course, that Sir Hamish is very seriously ill. How much hope there may be for him, how much time he has left, you know, that of course I can't say. What concerns me just a little is that at such a sad time there should be between them such a painful degree of marital tension. You must have noticed it yourself?

Davie: Oh, ay. Cannae miss thae things, can you, Jim? Sticks oot like a sair thumb.

Arbuthnot: Quite. I'm wondering, David, whether we couldn't do something to help them.

Davie: Dodgy business, that, Reverend, interfering between a man and his wife.

Arbuthnot: I know that, David. One would have to tread with very great care. But given the proper degree of disinterest — and you will note that I say *dis*interest, not uninterest — in the party working for reconciliation, something could perhaps be done to help them get back in touch with their own deepest feelings.

Davie: You'd be just the man for that, Jim.

Arbuthnot: Well, as a matter of fact, David, I was thinking rather of yourself.

Davie: Come oan, padre, you've got tae be jokin', you'd be landin' me in shit up tae my oxters, excuse ma French!

Arbuthnot: Hmm ... It may well seem to you that I'm shirking a responsibility that is proper to my calling.

Davie: Naw, naw, Jim, I wasnae sayin' that.

Arbuthnot: It would have been very understandable if you had been, though. But you see, David, nowadays we men of the cloth are often resented. I do not get the impression that Sir Hamish and Lady Cynthia are regular churchgoers, perhaps they are not even believers, at least in any formal sense. Now, you see, if I were to take on the role we have been discussing they might well suspect that I had an axe to grind, that I was exploiting their very sad situation unscrupulously, for proselytising motives. Do you see what I'm driving at? Whereas you have no axe to grind, you are truly disinterested.

Davie: Ay, well, I'm very sympathetic, like, tae their sityation an' that ...

Arbuthnot: Exactly! So you are doubly qualified. You feel for them, you are fond of them, I think, but you have no axe to grind. Are you with me?

Davie: *(doubtfully)* Ay ...

Arbuthnot: David, Hamish and Cynthia (I think we can now call them that) are running away from their feelings. They are seeking through confrontation to defend themselves from the onslaught of what is intolerable. They must be brought to understand that that is not the way. Only through facing their pain, facing it and sharing it together, will it be possible for them to overcome it, to triumph over it. They need to be helped, David, they need to be shown the way. What do you say?

Davie: I'm no up tae it, Reverend, honest.

Arbuthnot: But you *are*, David! Just rely on your instincts — you have an unusually fine gift of intuition. You have been given the opportunity to be a reconciler, David, a peacemaker. That is a very rare privilege.

Davie: When you put it like that, Jim, I cannae refuse.

Arbuthnot: *(shaking him warmly by the hand)* Excellent man!

Exeunt.

SCENE V

The following evening. Copenhagen — a pavement cafe.

Cynthia and Wee Davie seated at a table, both slightly drunk.

Davie: *(slightly apprehensive)* Wonder whaur Hamish has got to, then?

Cynthia: Oh, don't worry about him. Once he gets inside a museum he might be there for four or five hours. Anything that anyone else would find frantically boring, Hamish revels in. It's a kind of perversity.

Davie: Said he'd definitely meet us at six, though.

Cynthia: Hamish has no sense of direction. If he's supposed to go north-east, he'll go south-west. He'll get here eventually, don't worry.

Davie: He couldnae ha' taken a bad turn, like?

Cynthia: I doubt it. He's not that ill, not yet. A *wrong* turn, I think.

Davie: Must be awfae though, knowin' your number's up. Cannae help feelin' sorry for him.

Cynthia: Don't. If he sees that we feel sorry for him, he'll just feel even sorrier for himself. We have to make him forget about himself.

Davie: Ay, s'pose you're right.

Cynthia: Davie, I don't want to talk about Hamish, not tonight. As a matter of fact, I don't even want to think about Hamish. For the last twenty-seven years, I have has to think constantly about Hamish. Hamish's needs, Hamish's prospects, Hamish's career, Hamish's friends, Hamish's golfing weekends, Hamish's fishing, Hamish's socks! Tonight, I am on holiday. Hamish is not here. He will be here soon enough. Right now, Davie, you are here. You and I are here. Together. Let's forget about Hamish.

Davie: Ay. Fair enough. Like another beer?

Cynthia: I think we should have some schnapps, Davie, don't you? The wine of the country.

Davie: Ay, get intae the spirit of the north, eh, Cynthia? Fröken – two schnapps! Naw, naw, make it a bottle, hen. Ay. A bottle of schnapps.

Cynthia: Davie, I am just beginning to discover my own worth. Winning the competition, that was just the beginning. I can feel my untapped potential rising up in me like ... like sap! And you have been the ... the catalyst, Davie, that's the word! You're an alchemist, that's what you are — you are changing my base metal into gold!

Davie: Ach well, dae wur best, ken.

Cynthia: Isn't it amazing, Davie? Only two weeks ago you were just the man who sold us the doors — those doors that cost poor Hamish so much worry! If it hadn't been for Spot the Ball — thank God for Spot the Ball, Davie! Otherwise it might just have been me and Hamish and the Rev.Arbuthnot round the table. *(shudders histrionically).*

Davie: Ach, Jim's a' right, Cynthia. He's no bad. Heart's in the right place, ken.

Cynthia: Oh, *Jim's* all right, I'm not denying *that.* Skol!

Davie: Skol, Cynthia. You are a very wonderful woman. Don't sell yerself short, Cynthia. I seen a lot of women sell theirsels short. Nae good, that.

Cynthia: Did Marlene sell herself short?

Davie: Naw, widnae say so. No so's ye'd notice.

Cynthia: What was she like, Marlene? Or what *is* she like, I suppose I should say. Tell me about her.

Davie: See that Little Mermaid we seen this morning? Marlene was the very opposite o' that.

Cynthia: The opposite of the little Mermaid! How do you mean, Davie?

Davie: Marlene's a fish frae the waist up! *(roars with laughter)*

Cynthia: Oh Davie, you *are* an idiot! Tell me more.

Davie: No much mair tae tell, Cynthia. We were married nine year. Nae kids. Then she went aff wi' a real foul taxi driver ca'd Tommy Slattery. That's about it, ken.

Cynthia: You don't want to talk about her, do you? No. Any more than I want to talk about Hamish.

Davie: Hamish is a' right, though. Means well.

Cynthia: The worst thing you can say about anyone. That they mean well.

Davie: Ay. My granny used tae say that right enough. Slanjy vah.

Cynthia: Has there been anyone else, Davie? Since Marlene left, I mean. I'm not trying to pry.

Davie: *(embarrassed)* Ach well, juist a wee bit romp here an' there. Nothin' serious, ken.

Cynthia: If there *had* been someone else, I suppose she'd have been here with you, wouldn't she? And then where would I have been? Without my little alchemist! My strong, handsome little alchemist ... Oh, Davie!

Davie: *(apprehensive)* C'moan, darlin', gie's a break! Hamish could walk round that corner any minute.

Cynthia: Don't *mention* him, Davie. But *(drawing closer)* ... there's something I must tell you, darling. Since Hamish became ill — since the syntroms of the symbrome — *(giggles)* I mean the *symptoms* of the *syndrome* — gosh, I must be getting drunk! — anyway, since they began to appear, Hamish and I — you know, we haven't slept together. I don't mean *literally*, I mean we still *sleep* together, but there hasn't been, you know, any — sex.

Davie: Ay. My uncle had the very same trouble wi' my auntie, 's a matter of fact.

Cynthia: Really? How do you know? — Never mind. *(pause)* I just wanted to let you know that, anyway. *(long silence)* Davie, I don't know how to say this ... we haven't known each other more than a week — I mean, *really* known each other ... Oh, Davie, Davie, I want to feel you inside me!

Enter Sir Hamish, looking footsore and woebegone.

Sir Hamish: Sorry, people. I know I'm late.

Cynthia: Surprise, surprise!

Sir Hamish: I had plenty of time after I left the museum, so I thought I'd go and look at the statue, you know ...

Davie: The Little Mermaid, Hamish? We seen her this morning, no mind o' that?

Sir Hamish: No, no, Kierkegaard, the statue of Kierkegaard ... sorry, philosopher, nineteenth century religious philosopher.

Davie: Oh ay, auld Kirkyaird. That's the meaning of the name Kierkegaard, Hamish, did you know that? There's a lot of folk don't realise that.

Sir Hamish: *(surprised)* Yes ... yes, that's true. That is the meaning.

Davie: 'The despair of willing despairingly to be oneself'. Magic stuff, eh, Hamish? So — you got yourself lost?

Sir Hamish: *(wearily)* Yes — yes. I got there all right, but then — you know how it is in a strange city — I must somehow have taken a wrong turning. I was quite sure I was going in the right direction, walked miles and miles before I discovered my mistake ... Anyway, here I am. I feel desperately weary. You two seem to have been enjoying yourselves.

Davie: Oh, Cynthia an' I have been havin' a quiet little chat tae ourselves. Covered a lot of ground, eh, Cynthia? Here, have yersel a drink, Hamish. We're a long ways ahead of ye.

Sir Hamish: Thanks. Skol.

Cynthia: Davie and I have been discussing all *sorts* of things, Hamish. You would never guess how ... *far-ranging* our conversation has been. *(giggles)*.

Sir Hamish: Oh, I can imagine it all right. You are both born conversationalists, after all. And tonight, sufficiently well oiled.

Davie: We have been entering into the spirit of the country, Hamish, and of this beau'ful old town.

(Sings) Wonderful, wonderful Copenhagen,
          Salty old queen of the sea -
          Once I sailed away,
          But I'm back today ...

I've always liked that song, Hamish, thirty year before I seen beautiful Copenhagen I loved that song. Fuckin' magic. I would like to toast this fair city: 'Salty ol' queen of the sea!' Fuckin' wonderful. I admire that song ... I mean that ver' sincerely. Slanjy vah. Or Skol, should I say.

Sir Hamish: I can see that I *have* arrived a little late at the scene of rejoicing.

Cynthia: *(tipsily)* Yes, quite late, Hamish, you have arrived ever so slightly late.

Davie: I admire that woman. Speakin' personally, that is a very wonderful woman. An' I mean that ver' sincerely, Hamish ... a fuckin' wonderful woman, excuse ma Danish.

Sir Hamish: Oh, she's not so bad, it's true.

Cynthia: Such flattery! I am overwhelmed by all this flattery,

Davie: I'm glad you said that, Hamish. No bad. Speakin' personally , that is an understatement ... 'Scuse me, ah'm drunk.

Sir Hamish: *(ironically)* Really? How interesting. I've always wanted to meet someone who was drunk.

Cynthia: Oh, he's arrived all right, hasn't he Davie, Mr Smartypants has arrived!

Davie: Can ah say something? 'Scuse me, can ah say somethin'? That is the most fuckin' wonderful woman in the whole fuckin' world. ... Am ah speakin' outa turn?

Sir Hamish: *(frostily)* You've made your point, Davie. Cynthia is the most wonderful woman in the world. For the moment at least, that's agreed. Just for the sake of argument. Let's leave it at that, OK?

Cynthia: What a shit you are, Hamish!

Davie: No offence, Hamish! Awright? Nae offence!

Sir Hamish: OK, Davie, no offence. Discussion concluded. OK?

Davie: Put it there, Hamish ... Nae offence, pal, awright? ... Put it there! *(offers Hamish his hand. They shake hands)* That's ma pal, Cynthia. Greatest pal I've ever had in ma life. No kiddin'. 'S a matter of fact both of youse is ma pals. Know whit wad gie me very great pleasure? Know whit wad gie me very great pleasure? To see the baith o' ye's in harmony wi' wan anither ... *(attempts to put his arms around both)*

Cynthia: *(annoyed)* Oh, boak!

Sir Hamish: *(ironically)* Are you going to be sick, Cynthia?

Cynthia: *(slowly)* Yes, as a matter of fact, now that you mention it ... I think I am going to be sick ... quite soon.

Davie: Nae sooner said than done, eh Hamish?

Sir Hamish: Oh, God! Let's get her out of here! Davie, are you fit to travel? We'll have to find a taxi.

Cynthia: You stay, Hamish ... Davie and I don't need you ... Go back to Kierkegaard ... sing to mermaids ... stay here for ever ... Davie and I will get a taxi, won't we, Davie?

Davie: All go thegither, Cynthia — youse are baith ma pals ... Best pals I've ever had ...

Sir Hamish: Where is the bill? *(puts money on table)* You get on her left, Davie, we're going to have to support her to the kerb, there's bound to be a cab passing soon. Oh, good Lord, why am I here? Why did I come on this cruise? Why was I ever born? Never mind, I'll be dead soon.

They support Cynthia from the cafe.

Exeunt.

ACT II

SCENE I

The bar of the Saturn, the following evening.

Wee Davie is seated at the bar. Behind the bar, English barmaid, Sonia, aged about 25.

Sonia: Well, how are we this evening?

Davie: As well as can be expected, Sonia. That is, somewhat fragile, let us say.

Sonia: Had a lively night in Copenhagen, did we?

Davie: I would not quarrel with that description.

Sonia: A night to remember.

Davie: I would rather say, a night which it would be better tae forget. Can ah have a vodka' an lemonade, sweetheart?

Sonia: Vodka and lemonade, coming up. Things get a bit out of hand, did they?

Davie: Out of hand. I like that description. That expression would not be inaccurate as a description of what things got. Skol.

Sonia: Cheers, Davie. Tell us about it then.

Davie: *(confidentially)* See Sonia, there's this woman that's after me ... fancies me, ken ... got her claws intae me, like.

Sonia: What's wrong with that, Davie? You do like the lassies, don't you?

Davie: Oh ay, nae problem ... But this is trouble, Sonia ... She's married, like, rollin' wi' lolly, a toff an' that ... I'm outa ma depth, Sonia, honest.

Sonia: *(knowingly)* You don't mean Lady Cadfoot, do you? Never!

Davie: *(warily)* Ay, ay. Lady Cadfoot, Cynthia, like.

Sonia roars with laughter.

Davie: Its nae jokin' matter. I'm up tae my oxters,Sonia.

Sonia: Up to your what?

Davie: My oxters. Armpits, like.

Sonia: Oh I see, is that all. Well, stick in there, Davie. That's my advice.

Enter Rev James Arbuthnot.

Arbuthnot: Ah, David, there you are. I've been looking for you.

Davie: Hello there, Reverend. Lovely evening, eh? What're you drinkin, Jim?

Arbuthnot: No, no, thank you, David. I won't have anything. I'm going to get some air on deck before dinner, but I wanted a quick word in your ear if I may. *(draws him out of earshot)* How is it going, David? Your mission, I mean. Your office of mercy to our dear friends Hamish and Cynthia.

Davie: Softlee, softlee, Jim. I'm no rushin' it. Gainin' their confidence, like.

Arbuthnot: Yes, yes, of course. But we must not delay too long, we must strive for an early reconciliation. Cynthia, I thought, appeared deeply distressed today — you may have noticed how pale and puffy her face looked at breakfast, as if she had been weeping. The strain and anguish must be dreadful, of course.

Davie: Ay, ye can see that awright, Jim. An awfae strain.

Arbuthnot: It's obvious that Hamish is a very depressed man, and a very sick one, one just doesn't know how long he may have. It's tragic that man and wife should be at odds at such a time. Do what you can David. I count on you. Your reward will be great.

Davie: You're talking to Davie Cowmeadow, Jim. He's no lookin' for any reward.

Arbuthnot: No, no, of course not. And because you are looking for none, your reward will be all the greater. God speed. I shall see you at dinner, David. *(Exit)*.

Davie: Whhh! *(wipes brow)* Mair trouble, Sonia. Yon minister's got me workin' as a marriage guidance counsellor — for the Cadfoots like. Wants me to 'reconcile' them, nae less! And here's me tryin tae get away frae that Cynthia, oot o' her clutches, ken. I'm no up tae it, Sonia, honest I'm not. I'm just an ordinary sort o' boy — no intae that kinda stuff.

Sonia: You underestimate yourself, Davie. I'm sure you could cope with Lady Cadfoot no problem.

Davie: It's not just that, Sonia. See, her man's dyin' like, posterior-sacral redundancy syndrome, I cannae dae that tae him on his deathbed.

Sonia: Oh dear, that *is* sad. Still..he need never know, need he? And Cynthia's going to need consoling. Look at it this way, Davie — you've got something to offer her in her hour of need. If she wants it, and she doesn't get it from you, she's going to look for it somewhere else, isn't she?

Davie: *(uncertain)* Ay, well, I suppose ... there's somethin' in that, eh?

Sonia: And just think, when Sir Hamish dies — we don't want to think about that, of course, but we've got to be realistic — how long is he likely to live, by the way?

Davie: We're talkin' weeks here, Sonia. No months — we're talkin' weeks.

Sonia: Well then — when he *does* go, you're going to be around, aren't you, Davie? You're going to land on your feet, boy. You won't get another chance like that in your lifetime. What do you reckon they're worth?

Davie: Wouldnae like tae put a figure on it, Sonia, but we're talkin big money here. Nae doubt about that. Big money.

Sonia: Well, there you are, then. It's worth thinking about, isn't it? Worth a few minutes of cogitation? You think about it, Davie. And when you hit the big-time, remember who gave you a good piece of advice.

Davie: *(thinks for some time)* Did you ever hear o' a boy ca'd Peter Abelard, Sonia?

Sonia: Don't think so. Who is he?

Davie: Was, Sonia. He lived in the twelfth century, like. Great man. Great poet, great thinker, great lover.

Sonia: So what's he got to do with Lady Cadfoot, then?

Davie: Revolutionised morality, Peter Abelard. Said that sin was a' in the intention — no in the action, like. Ken whit I mean?

Sonia: No.

Davie: Right. Let's suppose I'm a married man, Sonia, an' I'm on this boat an I'm on ma way tae ma cabin for the night, get ma heid down, OK?

Sonia: Are you a married man, Davie?

Davie: Ay, well, only in a manner of speakin' ... but juist for the sake of argument, ken. Juist for the sake of argument, I'm a married man, OK?

Sonia: OK.

Davie: Awright. I'm on ma way tae ma cabin an' there's a power cut.

Sonia: Not very likely Davie. We've got our own generator, you know.

Davie: Naw, but juist for the sake of argument, like. C'mon Sonia, anything can happen in a storm. Right: I'm on my way tae ma cabin an' the lights gaes oot. I gaes in an' gets intae bed an' makes love tae my wife. Only, it's no my wife, it's you.

Sonia: It's me, Davie?

Davie: Ay. Juist for the sake of argument, like. Awright. Now, Sonia, before Peter Abelard, ye'd no find a theologian in the hale of Christendom that wouldnae say I'd committed adultery. You could look high an' low, Sonia, north and south, east an'west, an' ye'd no find wan that'd say I'd no committed adultery. No wan, Sonia. Nae way. You're not on. OK. Peter Abelard comes along: no, he says, the boy didnae commit adultery. See Wee David there, he says, he thought he was makin love to his wife. He wasnae, but he thought he was, so he didnae intend tae commit adultery. An' if he didnae intend tae dae it, then really speakin' he didnae dae it. Revolutionised morality, that.

Sonia: So you reckon that gives you *carte blanche* with Lady Cadfoot, do you?

Davie: Well, see, way I look at it, Sonia, I dinnae intend tae dae nothin' wrong wi' Cynthia. Sin lies in the intention, that's whit Peter Abelard says, an' I suppose he's right. So if I dinnae intend it tae happen, nae harm, eh? ... Mebbe Peter Abelard juist said that because o' whit he done tae Héloise, mind.

Sonia: What are you talking about, Davie?

Davie: Héloise was Abelard's pupil — juist a wee lassie, ken. He done her, and he got his balls chopped aff for his trouble.

Sonia: Wha-a- at? You're joking!

Davie: Naw, that's right though. See her uncle fancied her hissel, an' when he fand oot he had some boys break intae Abelard's digs, an' they fuckin' castrated him. Nae messin'. *(takes a handful of nuts)*

Sonia: A cautionary tale, Davie. But I shouldn't let it put you off. There's too much at stake.

Davie: Ay. What time is it? I'd better get away in tae my dinner. Say a prayer for me, Sonia. See wi' Cynthia on the wan side o' me and yon minister on the ither, I'm steerin' a gey dangerous course. Scylla an' Charybdis, eh? Devil an' the deep blue sea. It's no easy.

Sonia: No, Davie, but you'll win through.

Davie: *(takes another handful of nuts)* I'll keep ye posted, hen.

Sonia: Watch those nuts, Davie.

Davie: Ay. I'll dae that an' a'.

Exit Wee Davie.

SCENE II

The Dining saloon. The same evening.

Sir Hamish and Lady Cadfoot, Wee Davie and Rev. Arbuthnot at table.

Cynthia: Well, here we are again.

Arbuthnot: Yes, and time is passing. Already we are more than halfway through our little voyage. But there are good things still to come. Hamburg, and above all, Amsterdam.

Sir Hamish: I didn't think much of Göteborg. I got the impression initially that we were going to Stockholm, didn't you? Göteborg is scarcely a Northern Capital. Still, Copenhagen made up for it, I suppose. Though I found it exhausting.

Davie: See when we get tae Hamburg, will you be takin' us a tour of the Reeperbahn, Jim? I fancy samplin' the night life, hearin' a bit o' jazz an that. Don't get me wrong. I'll no be gaein' to nae brothels or nothin'.

Arbuthnot: Oh, I would like to take a look at the bright lights. No harm in that.

Cynthia: I shall leave all that to you men. I intend to do a little shopping and return quietly to the boat.

Sir Hamish: Everyone to their taste, that's what holidays are about. What wine are we having tonight — red?

Cynthia: I'd prefer white.

Davie: The lady wants white, we'll have white. What about a nice Chablis, eh? Nothin' tae beat a nice Chablis wi' Lobster Thermidore. Waiter! Two bottles of No. 16, thanking you.

Sir Hamish: That appears to be settled then. *(sighs and looks ill and unhappy)*

Long silence. The wine is brought and served.

Cynthia: We don't seem to be very good at conversation tonight, do we? The small talk is not flowing with its customary readiness. Why don't we play a game? Let's see: let's pretend we're all on one of those awful radio chat shows. We've all been asked to give our views on something really tedious. Let's see: we've all been asked to describe something that we really hate, something that gets up our noses.

Sir Hamish: One of us will have to be a psychologist, then. An English psychologist, of course, called something like 'Justin Fitton'. They always have one of those.

Cynthia: Well, that's as may be. We have to give our own opinion, that's the point, and we've got to be absolutely honest and truthful about it. Otherwise there's no point. Right. Hamish, you begin. Something you really hate. That gives you a wide range of choice.

Sir Hamish: *(sighs)* Misuse of the English language. In particular, people who use cant phrases and pompous circumlocutions in order to enhance their self-image, and then get it all wrong.

Cynthia: Predictable. Jim, can you come up with anything more thought-provoking?

Arbuthnot: I think, you know, that the one thing which I do find hard to stomach is intolerance. Intolerance is actually a form of aggression and very often, you know, it is a kind of *defensive* aggression. So often it is those whose self-esteem is lowest who are most self-assertive and intolerant. We must understand that and sympathise with it, of course, but at the same time it is not to be *condoned*. So many of the world's ills, I often feel, have at their root this terrible failing of *intolerance*.

Davie: So, ye can tolerate anything except intolerance, eh Jim?

Arbuthnot: *(a little taken aback, but chuckles)* Well, I dare say, you know, that there is some truth in that!

Cynthia: Right. So far we have misuse of the English language and we have intolerance. Right. My turn. What do I hate the most? I think ... I think ... People who beg for things. People who sit up on their hunkers and beg for things — to be admired, for instance. You know, those people who are for ever angling for compliments. If they would just come out and say 'Please compliment me', that would be all right. It's the *angling* that gets up one's nose. *(getting into her stride)* But even worse are people who beg for sympathy, in just the same sort of way, without ever coming out and saying 'Please feel sorry for me', putting on a show of stoicism and long-suffering. People who are ill are often like that, you know, especially people with fatal illnesses. *(with an increasingly mad look in her eye)* At first they try to bore you stiff with their symptoms, blind you with science, wear you down with unbelievably tedious descriptions of their yawn-making 'syndromes', trying to create a great *mystique* around their precious illnesses. But they find that there's a law of diminishing returns involved in that, no one can stand listening to that kind of thing for long, so then they put on the long face, never actually mention their boring syndrome but sigh all the time and look martyred, harp on about how tired they always are, carry on as if they might drop dead at any moment, and generally make themselves a pain in the backside. And all this is an underhand way of appealing for sympathy — sheer moral blackmail. I find that sort of thing absolutely disgusting and degrading. *(pause)* You must have met people like that. Odious.

Very long silence.

Davie: *(in a small, hurt voice)* Do I no get tae say somethin'?

Cynthia: Davie — yes — of *course* you do. Please tell us what *you* hate, Davie.

Davie: Ay, well. Know somethin that really scunners me? Know what really gies me the boak? Pickin' hairs aff a cake of soap.

Sir Hamish: *(roars with nervous laughter)* Davie! What a splendid man you are!

Cynthia: *(meditatively)* Yes. For once you have said something true, Hamish. All the rest of us were posturing, weren't we, each in his or her own way, talking for effect. Only Davie spoke from the heart.

Arbuthnot: 'Out of the mouths of babes and sucklings ... '

Davie: Come oan, Reverend! I'm no a babe, so what are you implyin' that I'm sucklin' at, eh?

Arbuthnot: *(highly confused)* Oh, good heavens, David, I'm not implying anything ...

Davie: *(gives him a playful punch on the arm)* I'm only kiddin' ye, Jim. *(looking out of the window and becoming meditative)* See a' thae big cranes, eh? It was tears that built the Clyde. *(Shakes head)*.

Sir Hamish: That's the Elbe, Davie.

Davie: Ay. Principle's the same, though.

Cynthia: How very right you are, Davie. The principle is the same. And it's principles that count, isn't it?

Davie: *(sadly)* Know somethin'? This woulda been ma wedding anniversary, if Marlene and I had still been together, like. Kinda melancholy, eh?

Arbuthnot: That is indeed a sadness, Davie. But you have nothing to reproach yourself for. It was Marlene who broke the sacred vows which bound you together.

Cynthia: Marlene didn't know when she was lucky. When you have a *good* man you should hang onto him. Imagine leaving you for that awful taxi-driver! I hope he batters her!

Davie: Ay, big Tommy Slattery. Big shitbag, eh?

Arbuthnot: There are always times when it is hard to honour one's vows, of course. Mrs Arbuthnot and I were blessed with great happiness, but even so there *were* times that were difficult. Oh yes. But 'for better or worse', you know, 'for richer or poorer' and, of course, 'in sickness and in health'. Oh yes, indeed. In sickness and in health.

Davie: Cannae say fairer than that, Jim.

Hamish starts to cry. Enter Captain.

Captain: So! Our happy party! I think you all have wonderful times on this voyage.

Sir Hamish: Is it that obvious?

Davie: Oh ay, Captain, we're a' gettin' on great here.

Captain: Good, good! And I have another piece of good news for you. May I join you for a moment? *(pulls up a chair)*.

Davie: Will you join us in a glass of wine, Captain? We are greatly enjoying your lovely Chablis.

Captain: Thank you, no, no, I am on duty. I come only to communicate glad tidings. The results of the General Knowledge Quiz are now available, and I am happy to say, Mr Cowmeadow, that you are the winner! So — you have won a half-gallon bottle of Scotch Whisky, and with it goes the title 'Brain of the Boat'! Congratulations, Mr Cowmeadow! First Spot the Ball winner, now Brain of the Boat!

Cynthia: Oh, Davie, that's wonderful! What a talented lot we are, aren't we — Glamorous Grannies and Brains of the Boat! Davie, you're quite a man.

Davie: No bad for an ordinary boy that left school at fifteen, eh?

Arbuthnot: I can testify to the extent and depth of David's theological knowledge, Captain. It far exceeds mine, I can assure you — though in all honesty mine is modest enough.

Captain: Where did you learn so much, sir? We are all so envious. Now. I have a little proposal. As you know, tonight after dinner we have Grand Ball. It is only a dance, really, but we call it Grand Ball. On this voyage, I hope that we have an innovation. It depends on you. Before commencement of the Ball, in a little ceremony we crown the King and the Queen of the good ship *Saturn*. After the coronation, the Royal couple will lead off the dancing — the first waltz. That is all. Now, who better to be our King and Queen than our Brain of the Boat and our most exceptionally Glamorous Granny? What do you say to my proposal? — I am in your hands.

Cynthia: Oh, Captain, of course — what an absolutely stunning idea! We'd love to — wouldn't we, Davie?

Davie: Cannae refuse — *noblesse oblige*, eh, Cynthia?

Captain: For such a function, beauty and brains present the ideal combination.

Davie: The brains — that must be you, Cynthia. 'Cos there's nae doubt that ah'm the beauty!

Cynthia: Oh Davie, you are an idiot! Gosh, I'm getting quite nervous already!

Captain: No need for nerves, Lady Cadfoot — it will not be hard. Just a good piece of fun, you know. I am so glad you consent.

Davie: Ye'll no mind, Hamish, if your good lady is ma Queen juist for tonight?

Sir Hamish: *(returns a gloomy, barely perceptible, lethargic, negative gesture).*

Captain: Good. So — I see the King and Queen in the Blue Lounge a little before the Ball commences and I go quickly over the details of the ceremony. It is very simple — no need to worry. No vows to be made! About half past nine, shall we say? Good. Until then.

Captain bows and Exit.

Cynthia: Well!

Arbuthnot: How privileged I feel to be sitting at this royal table!

Silence.

Sir Hamish: I suppose it would be quite useless for me to protest.

Cynthia: I was waiting for it. I was just waiting for it. I knew that it couldn't be long delayed, but I wasn't sure just when the moment would be. All right, Hamish. Make your protest. We are listening.

Sir Hamish: If the inexpressible vulgarity of the whole thing isn't obvious to everyone, then there is little point in my saying anything.

Cynthia: The inexpressible vulgarity! Well, excuse me! If His Lord High Wetblanketship says so, it must be right!

Sir Hamish: Cynthia, if you want to leave yourself without a shred of human dignity that is your concern. I have registered my protest and my conscience is clear. I would be failing to act as a husband should, were I not to attempt to warn you against making a degrading public spectacle of yourself. But the choice, of course, as always, is yours.

Cynthia: Why is it, Hamish, that when anything good happens to me you immediately have to do dirt on it? You just can't bear to see me in the limelight, that's what it is, even for one evening. If for even half an hour *you* are not the centre of attention, then nothing is right. If you were to be crowned King tonight it wouldn't be a 'degrading public spectacle', would it? But because its me, because it's Davie and me but especially because it's me, me and Davie, then it's all just so inexpressibly vulgar! You're a snob and a wimp, Hamish, a snob and a wimp.

Sir Hamish: *(with a hollow laugh)* I won't say any more. I shall not be there to witness the sorry spectacle. I won't say it's because I'm ill, because that would expose me to accusations of boring hypochondria, and I won't say it's because I'm absolutely dead tired, because then I would be accused of blackguardly moral blackmail and begging for sympathy. I simply won't be there.

Cynthia: Well, what an absolutely *crushing* blow! Davie, can we *possibly* be crowned in Hamish's absence? I mean, do you think it would even be legal?

Davie: Dinnae ask me, Cynthia, ah'm keepin' outa this — ma hands are clean.

Arbuthnot: Well, I must say, this is most distressing. Just a few minutes ago we were all so happy.

Cynthia: You keep out of this, you prating old faggot! Just because you're a minister, it doesn't give you the right to go poking your nose into other people's affairs when it isn't wanted, or to moralise from your lofty height on the faults of us poor erring mortals. Keep that for your sermons. *(Looks ostentatiously at her watch)* Davie, it's time we were getting ourselves ready for the ceremony. Excuse me.

Davie: It's no time yet, Cynthia ... *(she takes him by the arm and pulls him off)*. Ay, well then ... I'll see ye's later!

Exeunt Cynthia and Davie.

Short pause.

Sir Hamish: Jim, I apologise deeply on behalf of my wife. I don't know what else I can say.

Arbuthnot: Say nothing, Hamish, say nothing. I feel for you. I feel for you both profoundly. It seems that your illness is a cross that is too heavy for poor Cynthia to bear.

Sir Hamish: I had thought, Jim, that it was by no means a light one for me.

Arbuthnot: Of course, of course, please don't think that I am unaware of that ... But, you see, Hamish, it is a matter of 'we who are strong must bear with those who are weak'. That is never easy.

(considers for a moment) You know, you have a very great friend in David. You realise, of course, that he has — how shall I put it? — taken Cynthia's fancy. It is, of course, entirely innocent. It is not David as a man to whom she is attracted, you understand, it is David as the representative of Life. Instinctively, she turns away from Death and embraces Life. And David — God bless him — is using the advantage that gives him in order to help Cynthia recognise, and come to terms with, her feelings of rage — rage at this terrible illness which has come between you and which threatens — though God forbid that it should come to that — to tear you apart for ever. (I speak, of course, only of this transient world). David is helping her with that and it is a noble task.

Sir Hamish: Very good!

Arbuthnot: So, if David is successful, then you may find that things look very different in the morning. It may be that this crowning will prove ...

Sir Hamish: This crowning folly!

Arbuthnot: No, no, Hamish, don't look at it that way — it may be that this crowning will prove a turning-point, that it will mark the beginning of a new reign of peace and harmony in your lives. So I shall be praying, Hamish, that David is successful.

Sir Hamish: Hmm. So, no doubt, will he. *(pause)* Jim, I'm going to bed.

Exeunt.

SCENE III

The bar of the Saturn, later the same evening.

Sonia is behind the bar. Enter Cynthia and Wee Davie, both wearing crowns and both drunk, Davie more so. Davie is carrying a half-gallon bottle of whisky.

Davie: *(serenading Sonia)*

My, my oh my,
Gee, you're so fine
Don't let me down
I'm a king but you can wear my crown.

Hi there, Sonia darling, how're you daein? We're daein' fine.

Sonia: So I see. Coronation a success, was it?

Cynthia: Oh, it was marvellous. Just a fabulous evening from beginning to end! Wasn't it Davie?

Davie: *(singing)* ... A special paw'ry je' for you!

Cynthia sits down at a table. Davie goes up to the bar.

Sonia: *(aside)* I think you're on, Davie. Don't drink too much and mess it all up, now.

Davie: Don't you worry about a thing, Sonia, wee Davie's in control. Just gie's a coupla glasses, hen, we'll no be needin' a drink frae the bar wi' yon big bottle sittin' on the table.

Sonia: Well ... you're not supposed to bring your own drink into the bar but I don't suppose it matters at this time of night. I'll be closing the bar in a few minutes anyway. Perhaps you should take it to your cabin after that, eh?

Davie: Ay, that'll be right! Two glasses coming up, Cynthia.

Goes to the table with glasses, singing.

Everything's gonna be all right,
So be my guest tonight.

Cynthia: Oh, I could have danced all night! Oh, Davie, isn't it a night for clichés! It's just all been so magical. I feel I've shed thirty years in three hours. Don't you feel the same?

Davie: *(singing)*
                  When you are in love
                  It's the loveliest night of the year ...

(pours drink)

Cynthia: And it is the loveliest night of the year, isn't it? Just look at that moon shining out there, casting its pale beams over the towers and spires and turrets of old Hamburg, glinting on the waters, lighting up the cranes ... And if it's the loveliest night of the year, that proves we must be in love, doesn't it? As if proof were needed. Oh Davie, I haven't felt like this since I was eighteen. It takes me right back to the League of Pity Ball in the Assembly Rooms, way back in 19-- oh, I'd better not say nineteen-what, I'd be giving myself away, wouldn't I? I came up the stairs after supper, I'd just been powdering my nose, you know, I came round one of those huge pillars, and there he was, leaning nonchalantly against the pillar, smoking a Gauloise, just as if he didn't give a damn for anyone or anything ...

Davie: Auld Hamish, eh?

Cynthia: No, no, silly, Marcus Waddell-Farr! That was the beginning of the most passionate, tempestuous romance ... Hamish didn't come on the scene until that was all over. But don't let's talk about *him*, for God's sake. Tell me about your youth, Davie. Was there any romance in your youth that had that kind of quality — you know, that special something extra that seems as if it's not quite of this world?

Davie: *(thinking hard)* Eh well ... there was that wee bird I done down in the Isle o' Man, right enough ...

Cynthia: Tell me about her ... No, don't bother, I don't want to know about her, I want to pretend that you are in love for the first time, and so am I, that we're giving each other all the freshness of youth, all the aching sweetness of first love ... Davie, you're drinking too much, darling.

Davie: Dinnae worry about Wee Davie, sweetheart, he's a'ways in control.

Cynthia: Davie, we've got so much to face, so many dreadful problems awaiting us — some day soon that will all have to be faced up to. But tonight, let's just live for the moment, grab hold of happiness while we can, grab it with both hands. We're tragic lovers, aren't we, darling? Tristan and Isolde, Dante and Beatrice, — oh, I'm Héloise and you're Abelard ...

Davie: Sonia tellt me tae watch ma nuts, right enough!

Cynthia: I am Emma Bovary and you are — I forget who! No, no, you are Count Vronsky and I am Anna Karenina, that's it! I often used to be told that I was like Greta Garbo ...

Davie: Greta Garbo, eh? I get tellt I'm like Rab C. Nesbitt.

Cynthia: Rab C. Nesbitt? Oh, what nonsense — what a calumny! No, no you are Count Vronsky ...

Davie: Cunt whae?

Cynthia: Count Vronsky, my handsome, dashing, brilliant officer!

Sonia: I'm closing the bar down now, folks. I suggest that you take that to one of the cabins, there shouldn't be any drinking in the bar after it's closed. All right? Don't drink too much now, Davie, remember you have to be fit for Hamburg tomorrow!

Davie: G'night, darlin', see ye the morn.

Cynthia: Oh, thank goodness she's gone, I thought we were never going to be alone. I think we should take her advice, though, don't you, darling? Let's go to your cabin.

Davie: Ay, well ... we'll go in a minute or two, like.

Cynthia: Davie, you're drinking too much too fast, my love. *(comes up close to him and whispers)* Remember that you have important business to attend to tonight! *(they embrace)* Oh, Davie, Davie, I want you, I want you, I want to feel you inside me, now, I can't wait!

Davie: Ach, I know, Cynthia, I want you an' all — it's Hamish I'm thinkin' aboot, darlin'. See Hamish is ma pal ... I cannae dae that tae ma pal, an' him dyin' an' that ... it widnae be right, darlin' — he'll no be wi' us much longer ... Can we no juist wait till he's deid, Cynthia?

Cynthia: Oh Davie — that makes me love you even more — as if that were possible! What a noble nature you have! But ... no, darling, we can't wait for Hamish to die. He might live for months yet, even years — the doctors have never said that wasn't possible. Right now Hamish is snoring his head off — he's not going to know anything about it, is he? So it can't hurt him. Oh, what an old stick he is! — just like Anna Karenina's husband. Come on, darling, let's go to your place.

Davie: Ach, I don't know, hen — dinnae like tae dae that tae auld Hamish — 's ma pal, like ...

Cynthia: Oh, darling what a moralist you are! Can you imagine Count Vronsky saying that? And if he had Anna wouldn't have listened, and nor will I.

Davie: Ay, well, Anna endit up under the wheels of a train, mind.

Cynthia: Oh, you *morbid* moralist! Come on, Davie, we're going.

Takes him by the hand.

Davie: You win, Cynthia. *(grabs bottle of whisky)*

Exeunt.

SCENE IV

A bar in the Reeperbahn, Hamburg, the following evening.

Sir Hamish and Wee Davie are sitting drinking.

Sir Hamish: Well, so this is the Reeperbahn. Exciting, isn't it?

Davie: Bit ae a let-down, eh Hamish? Even the Reverend Arbuthnot woulda been quite safe here.

Sir Hamish: Yes — he chickened out of it , didn't he? What a transparent excuse — making out he wanted to keep an eye on Cynthia because she 'appeared to be unwell'! Unwell, indeed. And a few days ago he was all for it, he was going to go on the town by his way of it, 'savour the bright lights'! Huh!

Davie: Ay, that's the soft underbelly of the Scottish macho culture for ye, Hamish.

Sir Hamish: Yes. Well, we're just going to have to get drunk, Davie, you and I. *(pause)* Davie, I think you and I should have a talk, you know. I think we have a great deal to talk about, Davie.

Davie: *(warily)* Ay, Hamish?

Sir Hamish: *(settles himself for a lengthy discourse)* Davie, when one sees death approaching — you'll discover this yourself some day, not for a long time to come, I hope, but some day — one begins to ask oneself what exactly is important in life and what isn't. It's not a question of what *lasts*, no, no, because nothing lasts; it's a matter of what has *value,* you know, value that *speaks* to you when there's very little of life left to come — it speaks to you and says, *This* is worth while, *this* was not a total waste of time, *this* enhanced my wretched little life and lent it a little dignity. I have reached that point, Davie: I am asking myself these questions. The darkness is closing in on me faster with each day — I can feel it. So, I say to myself: what things in my life have that quality, that value, that precious, enhancing sense of worth? Career? No, not for me. At the end of the day I've done a good job and there's no more to it than that. Others may feel differently — not me. So: not my career. Material possessions? No, certainly not. Nice to have, yes I grant you, but that special quality? — no. Right. One's family. Now we're getting somewhere. Are you with me, Davie?

Davie: Ay, Hamish, I'm with you.

Sir Hamish: Good — good. One's family. My family. Little Samson. I would like to see little Samson growing up. His mother — my daughter Liz. I want to see her happy, successful, perhaps the mother of a larger brood. *(sighs)* Family love — a simple thing. What can one say of it? One doesn't need to say much — it simply has that quality. Do you understand what I'm saying, Davie?

Davie: Ay, Hamish, I ken juist what you're talking about.

Sir Hamish: Yes. Good. Family love. The love between husband and wife. My wife Cynthia. You know the score there, don't you Davie?

Davie: *(very warily)* Ay.

Sir Hamish: Yes. But, you know, there's something else that goes hand-in-hand with family love, which rounds it out, so to say, complements it, provides its background and establishes its context. Do you know what I'm referring to, Davie? No? I'm talking about *friendship*. Friendship: Yes. That has that quality, that *value*. When it's real, that is, only when it's real. And what are the qualities that make it real? Tolerance. Frankness. Give-and-take. Honest expression of opinion. And — what else? — yes: loyalty — that, I think, is the essence, that is what they call 'the bottom line'. Loyalty; trust. That's an even better word: trust. So simple. Don't you agree?

Davie: Ay, ye're right there, Hamish, there's truth in that.

Sir Hamish: You and I, Davie, now, we're friends, aren't we? True, we haven't known each other long, but these things aren't measured by time, are they? I think our friendship has these essential, defining qualities, doesn't it? Frankness, for instance, loyalty, trust? I think it has those?

Davie: Put it this way, Hamish — you're the greatest pal I've ever had — no kiddin'! *(increasingly desperate)* I mean that very sincerely! Greatest pal I've ever had in ma fuckin' life — put it there pal! *(extends hand to be shaken)*

Sir Hamish: *(suddenly cold)* Don't give me that, Davie. I know what happened last night.

Silence.

Davie: Nothin' happened, pal, honest. See, the way it was, Hamish ... ken, the whisky ... distiller's droop an' that? Know what I mean? Nothin' happened, pal — honest.

Sir Hamish: *(surprised and interested)* Really? You don't mean to tell me? Well ... That won't get you off the hook. Have you ever heard, Davie, of Abelard's theology of intention? I should think you would have heard of that, a well-read man like you. But just in case you haven't, what it says is that the sin lies not in the action but in the intention. Therefore, if you intend to commit a sin and are prevented from doing so by some, let us say, 'accident', the guilt of the sin remains with you. Get me?

Davie: Ay. *(a little resentful)* Where did *you* get tae know about Abelard's theology of intention?

Sir Hamish: I studied Medieval History at St Andrews University. Still, never mind, I've always wanted to be cuckolded, all my married life.

Davie: I've tellt ye Hamish — naething happened!

Sir Hamish: Well, well, I'm not one to bear a grudge. Cynthia was in need of a good shafting. Just a pity she didn't get it, that's all. Come on, let's have another drink.

Davie: Ay, let's dae that, Hamish. Nae offence, pal, OK? Put it there ... *(offers hand and Hamish accepts it)* ... You're the best pal ah've ever had, awright? Nae offence, pal.

Sir Hamish: God, what a hole this is! I hate Germany ... Look, there's a dwarf over there.

Davie: *(earnestly)* Funny you should mention that, Hamish. It's a little-known fact that there are more dwarves per capita of population in Germany than in any other European country. Except Bulgaria.

Sir Hamish: Really. *(musing)* I've always wanted to kick a dwarf, actually. Especially a German dwarf.

Davie: On ye go then, Hamish, ye're on yer holidays! That's whit ye come on yer holidays for, to dae everything ye'd like to dae! Gie him a bit kick, like. No to hurt him, ken, naw, naw, juist a bit kick. I'll get ye aff if there's trouble, I'll just say ye're a person of diminished responsibility — nae brain cells!

Sir Hamish: All right, I think I will. *(staggers over and kicks vaguely).*

Davie: Polizei! Kommen Sie schnell! I seen the boy kick a dwarf!

Sir Hamish: *(returning)* Dammit, missed. I'll just have to kick a Scottish dwarf instead — a Scottish poison dwarf!

Kicks wee Davie quite viciously — then slumps on chair, deflated.

Davie: *(completely shocked — silent for a few moments, then starts blubbering)* No like Wee Davie? He's a' right ... nae herm in him ... never dae ye a bad turn ... juist an ordinary Scottish boy, ken ... might lack the edyication of you folks ...

Sir Hamish: Oh, Davie, don't be like that! Stop blubbering! I was just being an idiot. Don't you know that it is those whom we love most that we are always tempted to kick hardest?

Davie: Is tha' right? Hamish, nothin' happened wi' Cynthia, honest ... I never meant nothin' tae happen, Hamish, that's why Wee Davie drunk sae much whisky, so's he couldna get it up! So you see, pal, the intention wisnae there!

Sir Hamish: Davie — is this really true?

Davie: Ay! Wee Davie drunk that much so's he widnae betray his pal ... *(starting to blubber again)* and then his pal kicked him!

Sir Hamish: Oh, Davie! *(long silence)* What have I done? What a swine I am! What a low-down, mean, miserable, unadulterated swine! How can you ever forgive me? How can I ever forgive myself? I had such despicable thoughts about you, Davie, I didn't even give you the chance to defend yourself, I assaulted you, I kicked you, and all along you had acted with the most irreproachable integrity! *(buries his face in his hands)* Oh, dear God!

Davie: Dinnae think twice about it, Hamish. Ye juist over-reacted. As a matter o fac', I think your reaction was a very human reaction, Hamish. Put it there, pal! *(they shake hands, then Sir Hamish falls on Wee Davie's neck, sobbing pitifully)* We're still pals, eh?

Sir Hamish: *(nodding)* Oh, Davie, Davie! The strain I've been under, the strain! To face death and betrayal together!

Davie: Very understandable, Hamish.

Sir Hamish: It's all coming out now. This is a great catharsis, Davie. I shall be all right in a moment.

After sobbing for a few moments longer, Hamish looks up at Davie with a wild look in his eye. Then he puts his hand on Davie's knee.

Sir Hamish: Davie — don't despise me — I've always admired you, from the first day we met, when you first came about the doors, I could tell there was something special about you. Then when you appeared on board — your panache, your style, your yachting cap! Oh, God, what am I saying? Davie, I may not have long to live ...

Davie: *(in alarmed apprehension, draws back)* Ye could be right there, pal!

Sir Hamish: *(slumps)* Oh, dear Lord, this is the end. Now I've shamed myself irremediably. Forget what I said, Davie, forget it as if it had never been, it wasn't me speaking, it was some devil ... No, you can't possibly forget it, can you? How could you? — This is the end, Davie: I think I shall die tomorrow — perhaps even tonight. *(sobbing again)* Davie, I don't want to die in Germany!

Davie: We'd better get back tae the ship, eh?

Sir Hamish: Yes, yes ... Davie, if I don't make it back to the *Saturn*, kiss Cynthia for me just once! No, no, not just once, kiss her again and again and again! Take her, Davie, she's yours for ever, I deliver her into your hands!

Davie: Are ye sure about that, Hamish?

Sir Hamish: Yes, I'm sure. I'm sure. I've just won a great victory in my soul, Davie — do you realise that? In my last hours I have found magnanimity, I have come upon it in some long-neglected corner of my spirit — I give Cynthia into your hands, my friend — take her ...

Davie: Well, if you're sure that's a' right — ye'll no regret it, Hamish, I'll look after her, pal ...

Sir Hamish: A great weight has been lifted from my mind ... But my strength is failing fast, Davie, we must get back to the ship. Help me to a taxi, my friend.

Exeunt.

Other **diehard** drama

Klytemnestra's Bairns, Bill Dunlop
Cutpurse/Once in Beaucaire, Bill Dunlop
Hare and Burke, Owen Dudley Edwards
Gang Doun wi a Sang, a play about William Soutar,
by Joy Hendry
Port and Lemon, the mystery behind Sherlock Holmes
/Laird of Samoa, John Cargill Thompson
Cheap and Tearful/Feel Good, John Cargill Thompson
*Hamlet II: Prince of Jutland/ Macbeth Speaks/ An English
Education,* John Cargill Thompson
Everything in the Garden and other plays,
by John Cargill Thompson
*What Shakespeare Missed/Romeo & Juliet: Happily Never
After/The Marvellous Boy/Cock-a-doodle-do!*
by John Cargill Thompson.
A Matter of Conviction/Parting Shot/When the Rain Stops,
by John Cargill Thompson
The Lord Chamberlain's Sleepless Nights, a collection
of plays by John Cargill Thompson

plays in latin

Alcestis & Medea by George Buchanan

SCENE V

The following morning at breakfast. The Dining Saloon.

Sir Hamish, Cynthia, Wee Davie and Rev. Arbuthnot seated at table.

Cynthia: Well, Jim, I am glad that we stayed on board yesterday evening, aren't you? I mean, look at those two. Would you like to be looking and feeling like they do, on a beautiful, balmy summer morning as we approach Amsterdam?

Arbuthnot: *(archly)* Well, no, I would not, Cynthia, but let us not be intolerant of human weakness. I am sure our two adventurers will rally soon and be fit to appreciate the beauties that still await us.

Cynthia: Hm. So how did you find the famous Reeperbahn, boys? All that jazz, the lurid night life, the risqué clubs, the sleezy brothels — did you do manly and virile things in the Reeperbahn, you dissolute pair of *roués*?

Davie: Naw, naw Cynthia, we done nothin' like that, honest, we juist got stuck intae the bevvy, like ...

Cynthia: I believe you, Davie, I believe you implicitly. Scottish machismo begins and ends with 'bevvy', as some of us have discovered.

Davie: *(apologetic)* We had a bit wander round an' that, but Hamish wasnae feelin' right, so we juist had a coupla jars an' picked up a cab, that was about it, eh, Hamish?

Sir Hamish: *(distracted)* Yes, yes ... It was a big, fluffy dog, a chow I think, I wanted to stroke it, to bury my hand in its thick fluffy yellow coat, and suddenly it snapped at me, I got such an awful fright ...

Cynthia: *(puzzled)* Where did this happen, Hamish? In the Reeperbahn?

Sir Hamish: Where? I'm not sure exactly ... somewhere in Morningside, I think ... It seemed such a big dog, it was almost level with my shoulders, but it looked so gentle, I never dreamt ... *(gazes blankly)*.

Arbuthnot: Is he unwell, do you think? Hamish, are you feeling all right?

Sir Hamish: *(groans)* Oh! ... Oh! ... I was standing just a foot or two away from it, I wanted to pat its head ...

Cynthia: Hamish, darling, look at me — are you all right? Oh God!

Sir Hamish: *(trembling and wide-eyed)* Then it opened its mouth, I caught a glimpse of its great red tongue, I could see almost right down its throat, its upper lip was curled back from its great sharp white fangs! ... AAAH! *(he lets out a strangled cry and slumps forward with his head on the table)*.

Cynthia: Oh, my God, no! Hamish! Hamish! Wake up darling! Jim, Davie, do something!

Arbuthnot: Get him back sitting up, David, lift him up — there! Oh, dear, dear! He's unconscious! Is it the syndrome, do you think, are these the symptoms?

Davie: That's the way my auntie was took, the verra same.

Cynthia: Oh Hamish, Hamish, please don't die, not now! You mustn't die among Dutchmen!

Arbuthnot: Waiter! Waiter! Sir Hamish has been taken ill! Come and help us!

Waiter rushes up and they try to revive Hamish. General consternation.

          Let me take his pulse, give me his wrist ... there *(takes pulse)*.

Cynthia: Oh, Jim, is it there, can you feel it? Tell me he's all right!

Arbuthnot: *(very grave)* We must get the doctor right away ... Waiter, get the ship's doctor at once, don't delay! *(Exit Waiter). (aside to Davie)* I can't feel a pulse.

Davie: I tellt him it was terminal.

Cynthia: Oh, God, Oh God, this can't be happening! Hamish, wake up!

Arbuthnot: I've come across this kind of thing before ... syncope.

Davie: He said it'd be last night or this morning, last night he tellt me like, he says, 'Davie,' he says, 'if it's no the night it'll be the morn's morn' ... Wisnae feelin' right.

Cynthia: Please help me! Someone, someone! Get Hamish to wake up, oh God, *please*!

Enter Ship's Doctor, with Waiter.

Doctor: Well, now, where's the patient? Ah good, you've got him sitting up again. Let's see now ... *(feels pulse, loosens Hamish's collar, produces stethoscope, rapid examination)*

Cynthia: Oh, doctor, tell me that he's all right!

Doctor: Was it sudden, the collapse, I mean? Were there any signs that it was coming on?

Arbuthnot: He started talking nonsense, doctor, something about being bitten by a dog — he seemed to be back in his childhood.

Doctor: Yes, yes, that could well be ... Right. Let's get him out of here and into a cabin, or somewhere where he can lie down ... we can carry him to the surgery, I think, it's not far. Yes. Now, gentlemen. Waiter, there is a stretcher in the surgery, please bring it at once. Thank you. Please be calm, Lady Cadfoot. Everything that can be done will be done, have no fear.

Cynthia: Please tell me that Hamish is going to live, doctor!

Davie: They say it's a completely painless death, Cynthia ...

The waiter returns with a stretcher. Sir Hamish is put on it and carried out.

Exeunt omnes.

SCENE VI

The deck, a short time later. Rev. Arbuthnot is pacing to and fro.

Arbuthnot: *(thinking aloud)* Now, I shall have to explain the special status of this service. 'This little Act of Remembrance', that would be the phrase, I think ... You will understand, of course, that this is not a funeral service, that will take place in Edinburgh, Hamish's home town, when we return to port ... This little Act of Remembrance is for the many who had become Hamish's friends over the past couple of weeks, here aboard the *Saturn*, the many who have come to know and love him ... No, perhaps 'love' is a bit strong ... Lady Cadfoot has asked me to say a few words. ... Some of his friends here may have known that Hamish was a sick man ... No, that might seem to imply that he liked to talk about it. Hamish Cadfoot knew that his time was limited ... the quiet courage with which he faced illness and adversity — yes, that's good. We need a more personal touch somewhere ... It's the little things, you know, that one remembers. Good phrase, but what *are* the little things that one remembers? Damned if I can think of any. Don't worry, that'll come, I shall think of something. Then there's the religious angle — that's tricky. Hamish may not have appeared to be — in a conventional sense — a religious person. Indeed, he would probably have roundly disclaimed any such description. And yet, you know, a man who attracts loyal friends is usually found to be rich in natural piety . That's excellent, links in with the theme of friendship, with David. The family should be mentioned first, though. Cynthia, his children: should I refer to little Samson? Not by name, perhaps, that might be going 'over the top' as they say. Anyway, the friendship theme: Perhaps the most striking thing about Hamish Cadfoot was his gift for friendship. He was a man of many friends, from all walks of life. Yes. And yet it is not the *number* of a man's friends that counts at the end of the day, it is their *quality*. Splendid. Now I can bring in young David at this point, his efforts at reconciliation — but hold on, there must be no suggestion of a marital rift: how can this be put? His support, his loving support, yes, that is fine and appropriate. A man who attracts loyal friends ...

Enter Wee Davie.

Ah, David — is there any further news?

Davie: No yet, Jim. The doctor's still with him, like. I cam away when he started his examination, ken. Didnae like tae butt in. Cynthia's in an awfae state.

Arbuthnot: *(sighs and shakes his head)* I pray to God that the end comes swiftly, David. It would be terrible if he were to remain unconscious for a protracted period. That would be dreadful for Cynthia — an awful, awful thing.

Davie: He tellt me to look eftir Cynthia when he was gone, Jim. Wi' his dying breath, like.

Arbuthnot: You don't mean to say he has spoken?

Davie: Naw, naw, last night it was. *(solemnly)* When he felt death approaching.

Arbuthnot: Ah, indeed? It's a solemn charge, David. A very great responsibility. Do you feel equal to the task?

Davie: Ach well, we'll dae wur best, ken.

Arbuthnot: I believe it can cause all sorts of difficulties, death at sea — legal difficulties, you know. Ah, well, we won't have to concern ourselves with that. *(pause)* Isn't it tragic, David, that they weren't able to complete this last holiday together? But we mustn't question the will of Providence.

Davie: No, you're right there, Jim. Wish that doctor'd come an' tell us how Hamish is doin', a' the same.

Arbuthnot: I couldn't feel any pulse, you know, David, none at all. I knew then there was no hope.

Davie: *(sighs)* The grim reaper, Jim. Comes tae us a'.

Enter Sir Hamish, Cynthia and the Ship's Doctor. Hamish is pale but looks happy, even joyful.

Arbuthnot: Merciful heaven! Hamish — you are alive — and well! Good heavens, can this be true?

Davie: Raisin' o' Lazarus, eh, Jim?

Sir Hamish: Yes! I believe I gave you all a bit of a fright! Don't remember anything about it, myself.

Cynthia: Isn't it wonderful? The doctor says there's nothing wrong with him at all — at least, not a great deal. Isn't he an old fraud?

Sir Hamish: It's true, you know — he says I could live to a ripe old age. Didn't you say that, doctor?

Doctor: Indeed, if you're careful and don't overdo things, there's no reason why you shouldn't live to quite a respectable age. At the moment we're just seeing how he does in the fresh air.

Arbuthnot: But — the syndrome? Do you not have the syndrome after all?

Sir Hamish: Oh, I've got it all right, but it seems I picked up the wrong end of the stick from my specialist. You know how it is when you're depressed and expecting the worst — you start assuming things, and then you misinterpret ... You see he told me that my condition was incurable, and I just understood that, you know, as 'fatal' — didn't occur to me at the time that incurable and fatal weren't necessarily the same thing. I *had* read that the syndrome was fatal, though, I'm sure of that ... ..

Doctor: No, Sir Hamish, postural-sacral redundancy syndrome never killed anyone!

Cynthia: Except Davie's auntie, so it seems!

Davie: Did ye say *postural*-sacral redundancy syndrome, doctor? *That's* no whit ma auntie had, naw, naw ... it was *posterior*-sacral redundancy syndrome, I'm shair o' that ...

Doctor: Ah yes, now that's a very different kettle of fish. You can die of that all right.

Sir Hamish: Good heavens, I believe it was the posterior variety that I read about! Never occurred to me that there could be two!

Cynthia: Oh, Hamish, what a preposterous, darling old fraud you are! But I love you. *(kisses him on the cheek)*

Davie: *(half to himself)* This isnae real.

Sir Hamish: But, doctor, there was an operation Fraser spoke about, which he advised me not to have — I understood it was a life-or-death affair, terribly unpredictable in its outcome ...

Doctor: Oh, that must be the procedure to reduce pressure in the oesophagus, it can ease the symptoms a bit. But it is true that it often does more harm than good, that's probably what your specialist was saying. I expect you've been elaborating the whole thing again in your imagination. It often happens.

Cynthia: But doctor, is he likely to get these attacks often?

Doctor: Oh, no, I shouldn't think so. This attack had nothing at all to do with the syndrome. It's the result of overwrought nerves compounded with excessive consumption of alcohol over a period of several days. Forgive my frankness. Basically, he just fainted.

Arbuthnot: But the pulse — I couldn't detect a pulse at all!

Doctor: Oh, that's not surprising. It can be very hard to detect the pulse, especially if you're not used to taking it.

Sir Hamish: I feel marvellous! Absolutely marvellous!

Cynthia: Oh, this calls for a celebration! Let's all get drunk!

Davie: No real!

Sir Hamish: *(holds up his hands in mock outrage, but laughing)* Oh, no! Oh, dear me no — no alcohol for me for quite a long time to come. Doctor's orders. Isn't that so, doctor?

Doctor: *(frostily)* A period of abstinence would certainly be advisable. Well, if you will excuse me. I shall visit you in your cabin this evening, Sir Hamish — about six thirty? Meanwhile, take things easy.

Exit.

Arbuthnot: Well, I am somewhat dazed by all this. But what wonderful news it is — eh, David?

Davie: Ay, I'm pretty fazed masel, Reverend. But may I be the first to offer ma congratulations, Hamish — an' I mean that very sincerely. Long life an' happiness — put it there, pal.

They shake hands.

Sir Hamish: Davie, you are a sweet man.

Cynthia: I want to do something wild and crazy! I don't know what, though, leap into a canal in the middle of Amsterdam with all my clothes on! — something like that.

Sir Hamish: No Amsterdam for me today, I'm afraid, the doctor said I wasn't to go ashore. And to tell the truth, my legs feel a bit wobbly again. Think I'll spend the day in a deck-chair.

Cynthia: Never mind, darling, we've got another day — tomorrow we'll all go to Amsterdam and — get drunk!

Davie: *(sings)*

> When it's spring again I'll bring again
> Tulips from Amsterdam ...

Cynthia: Oh Davie, do stop that awful noise, you have no sense of *occasion* ...

Exeunt omnes.

SCENE VII

The Deck. Two days later.

Enter Sir Hamish and Cynthia.

Sir Hamish: Well, darling, here we are. Leith Docks. Home again ... like waking from a nightmare.

Cynthia: Oh no, Hamish, a dream, a beautiful dream! Who would have thought when we set off that I'd end up the most Glamorous Granny *and* Queen of the Ship?

Sir Hamish: Quite something, dear. I'm very proud of you.

Cynthia: And then of course your wonderful news, darling ... All that worry though ... it's helped us to get closer, hasn't it dear?

Sir Hamish: Why ... yes ... yes, I suppose it has. Have you said goodbye to everyone?

Cynthia: Well, let's see ... we've done the minister — what an old drone he is, isn't he? I thought we were *never* going to get away from him. What a prosing old moralist!

Sir Hamish: Yes, imagine having *him* conduct your funeral service! Still, he means well. We must have a word with Davie, though. I'm almost going to miss him, you know. After all we said about him at the start.

Cynthia: He's a funny little chap, isn't he? Quite sweet, in a way.

Sir Hamish: Yes – he's quite a character, you know. There's a poetic side to him, almost. He's actually rather fun — in small doses.

Cynthia: Yes — he is, actually. Still, it'll be good to be by ourselves again, won't it? Just the two of us.

Sir Hamish: Look, darling, there's Liz waiting for us — you see, over there beside that tall man in the blue anorak — yes — and little Samson — she's got little Samson with her!

Cynthia: Oh! Look, darling — he's waving! Little Samson is waving! Bless his little heart! He's waving at his Glamorous Granny! Hooee! He-llo, Samson! Who loves his granny?

Enter Wee Davie.

Davie: Well! There we are, then — Home Sweet Home. The time has come, as they say.

Sir Hamish: Davie! We were just talking about you — worried we were going to miss you. Davie, it's been great sharing a table with you. It has so much enhanced our enjoyment of the whole trip. Thank you.

Davie: It's been a memorable trip, Hamish, has it no? There'll be many a reminiscence at the fireside on the long winter evenings, I'm shair o' that. Put it there, pal. *(they shake hands)* Cynthia — ma Queen for a night. What can I say?

Cynthia: Say nothing, Davie. Farewell, sweet prince. *(She offers her cheek to be kissed. Davie kisses it)*

Sir Hamish: *(clears his throat)* Well, Davie ... Don't know when we'll be seeing you again.

Davie: Ay, well, let's see sir ... Young Stuart plays pool on a Monday ... it'll likely be either Tuesday or Wednesday of next week, sir ... We'll get thae doors hung for ye, nae bother ... If it's no Tuesday it'll be Wednesday, that's a promise!

(Curtain).